Forty Years of Intentional Excellence

Forty Years of
Intentional Excellence

The History of the Center
for Leadership Development

Julie Young

Printed in Mexico

This book is a publication of the Indiana Historical Society Press
Eugene and Marilyn Glick Indiana History Center
450 West Ohio Street, Indianapolis, Indiana 46202-3269 USA
http://www.indianahistory.org | Telephone orders 1-800-447-1830
Fax orders 1-317-234-0562 | Online orders @ http://shop.indianahistory.org

Library of Congress Cataloging-in-Publication Data

Names: Young, Julie, 1972- author.
Title: Forty years of intentional excellence : the history of the Center for Leadership
  Development / Julie Young.
Description: Indianapolis : Indiana Historical Society Press, 2017. | Includes bibliographical
  references.
Identifiers: LCCN 2017033320 (print) | LCCN 2017044474 (ebook) | ISBN 9780871954237
  (epub) | ISBN 9780871954220 (cloth : alk. paper)
Subjects: LCSH: Center for Leadership Development (Indianapolis, Ind.) | African American
  youth—Services for—Indiana—Indianapolis. |Minority youth—Services for—Indiana—
  Indianapolis. | Minorities—Vocational guidance—Indiana—Indianapolis. | Minority
  business enterprises—Indiana—Indianapolis. | Leadership–Study and teaching—Indiana—
  Indianapolis. | Community development—Indiana—Indianapolis.
Classification: LCC HV1437.I6 (ebook) | LCC HV1437.I6 Y68 2017 (print)
  |DDC 362.71—dc23
LC record available at https://lccn.loc.gov/2017033320

The paper in this publication meets the minimum requirements of American National
Standard for Information Sciences—Permanence of Paper for Printed Library Materials,
ANSI Z39. 48–1984

To all who have supported and sustained CLD through the past forty years of service to thousands of Indiana youth and families. As we celebrate this momentous point in CLD's history, we do so by honoring all of the community leaders, volunteers, and donors who have guided CLD from concept to reality. A special thank you to our visionary and founder S. Henry Bundles Jr. We also give thanks to the gentlemen who demonstrated leadership and tireless dedication by serving as chairmen of the board of CLD: the late Schuyler Otteson, Jerry D. Semler, Stephen A. Stitle, Doctor Robert L. Bowen, and Thomas A King.

We leverage this outstanding leadership in remaining steadfast in our commitment to inspire and develop African American youth for college, career, service, and life achievement. As we look forward, we seek to engage CLD alumni, stakeholders, and partners in developing CLD into one of the most preeminent youth-development programs in the country. We express our gratitude by working diligently each day to continue to make this vision a reality. We thank you for your trust.

Funding for this project was provided by an anonymous CLD board member. On behalf of CLD, we thank them for their generous contribution.

 *Principles for Success*

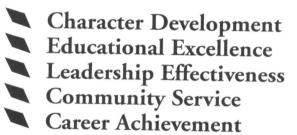

Character Development
Educational Excellence
Leadership Effectiveness
Community Service
Career Achievement

Contents

Center for Leadership Development Timeline   viii

Introduction   1

1 The State of the Union, 1976   3

2 The Center for Leadership Development's Mission and Vision Is Born   11

3 Self-Discovery/Career Exploration Project   21

4 Building Bonds, Acknowledging Achievement   29

5 Growing with the Times   39

6 Passing the Torch   47

7 A New Home   53

8 The College Prep Institute   61

9 The Impact of the Center for Leadership Development   69

10 A Vision of the Future   75

Conclusion   83

Bibliography   87

Center for Leadership Development Timeline

October 1976: Founding board members meet at the Indianapolis Athletic Club to decide on a name for the organization and to draft a job description for the president's position.

January 1977: Articles of incorporation are executed and certified. Henry Bundles is installed as the first president of the CLD by unanimous vote. Schulyer F. Otteson is named chairman of the CLD board of directors.

September 1977: First CLD classes are held in the Eli Lilly and Company A-Frame Boy Scout Building at Merrill and New Jersey Streets. There are ten sessions to the program.

January 1978: First Minority Business in Action seminar is held.

March 1978: First CLD graduation ceremony is held with 109 students receiving a certificate of completion.

April 1978: CLD alums take the first of many bus trips to Indiana University, Bloomington.

July 1978: CLD offers a six-week advanced program designed to help students secure summer employment.

August 1978: CLD revamps its Youth Development program to include material from the advanced course and extends the program from ten to thirteen weeks.

1980: CLD partners with Indiana University–Purdue University at Indianapolis to offer a six-week Scholastic Aptitude Test prep program.

March 1981: CLD holds the first Minority Business and Professional Achievers Recognition Awards Dinner at the Indianapolis Convention Center 500 ballroom.

1982: CLD relocates its classrooms and administrative offices to the Stutz Building at 1036 North Capitol Avenue.

1987: CLD celebrates its tenth anniversary and introduces the Business Orientation Project.

1988: Jerry D. Semler is named chairman of the CLD board of directors. CLD relocates to Methodist Health Foundation Building at 1812 North Meridian Street.

March 1988: First year in which a CLD alum, Everette Greene, is nominated for the Business and Professional Achievers Recognition Awards.

1991: Project MR (Male Responsibility) program is launched.

1995: CLD relocates to new facility at 3536 Washington Boulevard. Parent's Chat program is launched.

1997: CLD celebrates its twentieth anniversary.

1999: Stephen A. Stitle is named chairman of the CLD board of directors

2000: CLD founding president Henry Bundles retires and Dennis Bland is installed as the new president.

2002: Rawls Scholars Medicine Initiative is launched.

2003: Success Prep program is launched.

2004: Imani Book Club is launched.

2006: Robert L. Bowen is named chairman of the CLD board of directors

2007: CLD celebrates its thirtieth anniversary and receives a $1.4 million grant from Eli Lilly and Company for a new state-of-the-art building on Doctor Martin Luther King Jr. Street. Precious Miss program is launched.

October 3, 2007: Groundbreaking ceremony for the Lilly CLD Achievement Center is held.

2008: Junior Self-Discovery/Career Exploration class is offered to fourth to sixth graders.

April 13, 2009: CLD holds ribbon-cutting ceremony for the Lilly CLD Achievement Center at 2425 Doctor Martin Luther King Jr. Street.

September 12, 2012: CLD College Prep Institute Launch and ribbon cutting is held.

May 2013: Thomas A. King is named chairman of the CLD board of directors.

2014: Former CLD Young Adult Advisory Board member Amos Brown hosts CLD Day on his radio talk show *Afternoons with Amos*.

January 3, 2017: CLD celebrates its fortieth anniversary.

Introduction

"In order to get there . . . you must start here."

Human potential, like the universe, is constantly expanding. Giant leaps in business, technology, science, and engineering have been not only significant in propelling man outward, but also in helping to solve many of the problems that exist here on Earth.

In order to continue making great strides in technology, and at the same time make our world a better place in which to live, it is important to develop the most abundant resource that we have—people.

In Indianapolis, Indiana, there is an organization that is charged with developing the human resources of a specific population segment. It is called the Center for Leadership Development. Conceived in the mind of a visionary business-man and built in cooperation with Lilly Endowment and the Indiana University School of Business, the CLD is dedicated to improving the quality and quantity of minorities in business and the professions through programs for minority youth, minority professionals, and the recognition of minority achievers across a broad spectrum of fields.

This is the CLD story.

> "People will succeed if you give them the opportunity."
>
> *Jim Morris*

Chapter 1 The State of the Union, 1976

When the United States reached its bicentennial, there was hope among the nation's leaders that the momentous occasion would restore a sense of unity among Americans still reeling from the Vietnam War, Watergate scandal, and the cultural upheaval of the 1960s. As patriotic parades, festivals, and celebrations were planned in communities all across the country, President Gerald R. Ford believed that America's biggest birthday was just the kind of event that could bring people together.

"For two centuries, our nation has grown, changed and flourished. A diverse people from all corners of the Earth have joined together to fulfill the promise of democracy. . . . The Bicentennial offers each of us the opportunity to join with our fellow citizens in honoring the past and preparing for the future in communities across the nation," Ford said in his official statement.

However, not everyone felt compelled to celebrate. Although the State of the Union was better than it had been only a year before, the American people were still struggling. The nation's unemployment rate was nearly 8 percent. The cost of goods was too high, sales were too low, and government spending remained out of control. By the year's end, the federal deficit would be $73.7 billion, the national debt would swell to $620 billion, and the United Sates would still be dependent on others for essential energy.

In addition to the problems facing everyone, there were those who wondered if the country should be celebrating anything at all. Members of the African American community, Native American tribes, and other minority groups were ambivalent about feting a nation that did little to promote them over the years. Historical injustices were bad enough, but despite the advances in civil rights and minority inclusion, there remained a disparity between white and nonwhite groups that permeated every aspect of American life.

Demographic Discrepancies in the United States

MEDIAN FAMILY INCOME IN 1976: $14,960

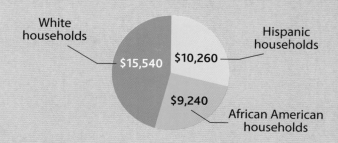

White households — $15,540

Hispanic households — $10,260

African American households — $9,240

UNEMPLOYMENT RATES

U.S. unemployment rate, 1976: **7.7 percent**

Overall unemployed American men, 1970: **3.8 percent**

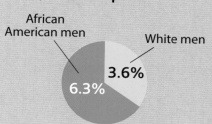

African American men — 6.3%

White men — 3.6%

Overall unemployed American women, 1970: **5.2 percent**

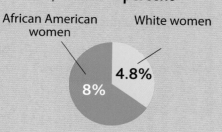

African American women — 8%

White women — 4.8%

Overall unemployed American men, 1980: **6.5 percent**

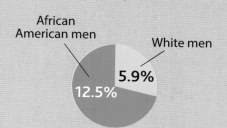

African American men — 12.5%

White men — 5.9%

Overall unemployed American women, 1980: **6.5 percent**

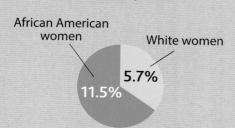

African American women — 11.5%

White women — 5.7%

EDUCATION LEVELS, 1976

High School Completion

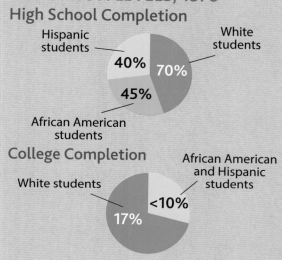

Hispanic students — 40%

White students — 70%

African American students — 45%

College Completion

White students — 17%

African American and Hispanic students — <10%

HOME OWNERSHIP, 1976

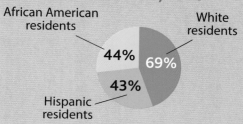

African American residents — 44%

White residents — 69%

Hispanic residents — 43%

AMERICANS LIVING AT OR BELOW THE POVERTY LEVEL IN 1975: 11.8 PERCENT

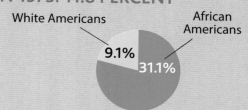

White Americans — 9.1%

African Americans — 31.1%

Local issues

Indianapolis was not immune to the injustices faced by minorities across the nation. Although African Americans living in the Circle City enjoyed the highest level of home ownership, educational attainment, and per capita income compared to similarly sized cities in the Midwest, it was not equal to that of their white counterparts. Racism and discrimination prevented African Americans and other minorities from enjoying a wide range of opportunities afforded the white community. While there were some African American leaders in business and industry, approximately 85 percent of black adults spent most of their post-secondary years in blue-collar fields—fields that may have provided decent benefits and enough money to get by, but offered little in the way of job security or advancement.

To make matters worse, many of these jobs were being eliminated. Since the late 1960s American manufacturing had been on the decline, and it was changing the landscape of the Midwest. Factories that were once counted on by both black and white workers to provide good jobs, solid salaries, and stable communities were reducing their work-force, moving their operations, or closing alto-gether, creating a ripple effect in the surrounding neighborhoods.

At one time, RCA Radio/Television employed 8,200 men and women at its facility on Sherman Drive. However, in the 1970s the plant cut its production

line to the minimum before relocating to Bloom-ington in the 1980s and eventually Mexico. Manu-facturing along the Shadeland Avenue corridor stalled as well. In the 1960s Western Electric had more than 9,000 employees at its bustling plant on the east side, but as demand for telephones dropped off over the next two decades, only 3,800 remained when the building closed in 1983. Some of the employees were transferred to other

plants, but others had to look for new positions elsewhere. Things were no better across the street at the Chrysler Electrical Plant. Although the firm had once employed more than 3,000 United Auto Worker laborers on site, permanent layoffs and transfers occurred throughout the 1970s until the campus was shuttered a decade later.

As the trend continued, new opportunities emerged, but these new opportunities were the

Downtown Indianapolis, 1970s

5

James Morris

jobs of the 1980s: suburban, knowledge-based positions that rewarded the highly educated and were supported by the low-skill, low-wage service worker. These emerging fields had a huge impact on those people who relied on the previous model for their livelihoods, such as the post-secondary African American community that was still largely marginalized and overlooked by the rest of society.

Those who could make the transition did. They went to college, got their degrees, and moved to the suburbs to make a new life for themselves. Those who had business interests and an entrepreneurial spirit rolled up their sleeves and pushed

against the tide to help their businesses grow and flourish. But those who did not struggled with the technology shift, shrinking opportunities, and neighborhood decline. Without a post-secondary education, proper preparation for the emerging job market, a transferable skill set, and visible role models, minorities faced a narrow economic outlook. It was a trend that could not continue, and in 1976 someone decided to do something about it.

Bundles Seeks a Solution

S. Henry Bundles Jr. was only sixteen years old when he saw the slogan that helped to shape his

Students at Crispus Attucks High School

IHS, *INDIANAPOLIS RECORDER COLLECTION*, P303

Crispus Attucks High School

life: "Don't tell what you do . . . make what you do tell." It was a nondescript sign hanging on the wall of a World War II defense plant, but its simple message struck a powerful chord with the young man and had a huge impact on his future career.

Born in 1927, Bundles was a 1943 graduate of Crispus Attucks High School who was on the cusp of an exciting future, even if he did not know it yet. After receiving his diploma, he enrolled at Indiana University with plans to study journalism, but was drafted to serve in World War II. He completed a tour in Hawaii and when his initial enlistment was over he returned to the Bloomington campus and earned his degree in 1948.

During his college career, Bundles associated with a wide circle of progressive people who thought highly of him and treated him as an equal, but he was no stranger to the kinds of discrimination African Americans in Indianapolis regularly faced. After graduating from IU, he applied for a position with the *Indianapolis News* and was thrilled when he was hired. However, his enthusiasm waned when he realized he would not be working in the bullpen with the other reporters. Instead, he was given a job as a district circulation manager overseeing a group of paperboys who delivered the afternoon edition along neighborhood routes.

Undeterred, Bundles went on to become a staff writer for the *Pittsburgh Courier* (Chicago edition), served another tour of duty with the military during the Korean War, married A'Lelia Mae Perry in 1950, and became a sales representative for the Apex Hair Company in Atlantic City, New Jersey, all before his thirtieth birthday.

In 1955 Bundles returned to Indianapolis with his family to become a sales manager for the legendary Madam C. J. Walker Company and eventually the president of Summit Laboratories. These two entities were the most successful minority-owned manufacturing businesses in the city, and under Bundles's leadership the latter would go on to

Henry S. Bundles Jr. (center) at WLIB Radio

become one of the top fabricators of ethnic hair products in the country.

Unfortunately, little in Indianapolis had changed. Bundles settled his family in a typical middle-class, African American neighborhood populated by two doctors and a host of other professionals only to discover that city officials had redlined it as a risky investment for economic development. (Redlining helped intensify the decline of these same neighborhoods for decades to come.)

Bundles also noticed a continued lack of diversity in the city's business community, something he longed to change. He became active in a number of civic organizations and cultivated an expansive network of like-minded friends who met during the turbulent 1960s to improve the integration of African Americans into the Indianapolis business sector, fraternal organizations, and service clubs that had previously been closed to them.

In 1968 Bundles received a call from Jim Morris, an administrative assistant for Mayor Richard Lugar, who asked Bundles to chair a committee on black capitalism. Morris knew Bundles had encouraged the promotion of African Americans to positions of prominence, which helped the Circle City remain calm when riots erupted elsewhere, and he also knew there was more to be done. After hearing Morris's proposal, Bundles accepted the appointment and became the first chairman and president of the Minority Business Development Foundation.

"Henry has been my friend forever. He was a civic activist, a respected businessman and was running a successful company," Morris said. "Henry was a

terrific guy who was funny, smart and cared deeply for the community. He was the perfect person for the job."

Fostering Future Talent

The Minority Business Development Foundation was a community action organization funded by the Lilly Endowment and private donations that was committed to the creation and expansion of minority-owned businesses in the Indianapolis area. The group was determined to combat community deterioration by widening the economic base of the city, providing professional development opportunities, advising those with business interests, and providing capital seed money so that entrepreneurs could qualify for traditional bank loans.

"We think this new project will create a new breed of spokesmen for Negroes and a new level of participation in the black community," Bundles said at the time of the MBDF's inception.

However, he realized it was not enough to support minorities who were already engaged in the business sector or those with entrepreneurial ambitions. There was also a need to develop future talent. By the mid-1970s it became apparent to Bundles and the other community leaders that there were several cultural and institutional barriers prohibiting or severely limiting minority youth from achieving academic and career success. They did not value education as an aspirational goal, they were not aware of the opportunities available to them, they did not have the support of their educators and community, and there was a lack of visible

African American role models willing to step up to guide them.

It was this knowledge that led Bundles to what he described as his most rewarding endeavor—one that would give young men and women a new model for success, help them discover who they were, "make what they do tell," and advance the next generation of trailblazers: the Center for Leadership Development.

"Don't tell what you do . . . make what you do tell."

Chapter 2 The Center for Leadership Development's Mission and Vision Is Born

Once he understood the barriers preventing minority youth from graduating high school, seeking a college education, and achieving a personally rewarding career, Henry Bundles was determined to reverse the trend. In 1975 he approached Melvin Woods of the Lilly Endowment and Doctor Jack Wentworth of the Indiana University School of Business for their help in creating a feasibility study on the potential to improve the quality and quantity of minorities in business and industry. When the results of the study agreed with his assessment, Bundles put his plan into action. The result was the Center for Leadership Development.

Organized in 1976 and founded on January 3, 1977, the CLD was designed to foster the advancement of minority youth in central Indiana as future professional, business, and community leaders by providing experiences that encouraged professional development and educational attainment. A board of directors comprised of leaders in the business community, minority organizations, and the educational field was created to govern the organization and to hire a president to oversee the CLD's day-to-day operations. It was important to find a sensitive individual who could analyze the needs of young people in the community and create a program that would meet the CLD's educational goals.

He or she must be able to help establish the CLD's credibility within the minority community while developing the kind of organization that would also encourage the support of the larger public.

Throughout the fall of 1976, the board culled though a number of applicants and decided to formally interview five candidates. Each person had unique qualities that would bring value to the CLD, but one name stood out from the others. On January 4, 1977, the board met and voted unanimously to offer Bundles the job, and he happily accepted the position.

The following persons are assisting in the development of our Youth Program.

DIRECTORS OF GUIDANCE & CAREER EDUCATION
INDIANAPOLIS PUBLIC SCHOOLS

Dr. Patricia Alexander
Gaylord Allen
Jack Brown
Frank Chase
Darryl Cork
Gene Critchfield
Marilyn Dearing
James Dozier
Juan Gant
Mahershall Gardner
William Harrison
Barbara Hine
Dr. Waldo Hoffman
Victor Johnson
Robert Ludlow
George Posey
Roselyn Richardson
Dan Rogers
Dr. Judith Samuelson
Eleanor Smith
Tom Totten
Linda Twines
Jonn Vardaman
Dan Welch
Dr. Belgen Wells
Jackie Williams
Eunice Willis
Betty Garrett

EDUCATION CONSULTANTS

Martha Mitchell
Nancy Shaw
Marcella Taylor

YOUNG ADULT ADVISORY COUNCIL

John Bailey
Anthony Barnett
Michael Barnett
Tom Batties
John Brooks
Amos Brown
Lance Bundles
Marilyn Christian
Robert Collins
Robert Conn
Clintina Cooper
Juan Craig
R. David DeFrantz
Dr. Harold Ervin
Dr. Steve Gordon
Holbrook Hankinson
Riley Lloyd
Bobbie Lyons
Nickey Morris
Bill Petty
Denise Ramsey
Yvonne Rawls
Lodia Richards
Mary Richards
Ben Singletary
Perry Washington

*   *   *   *   *

The Youth Development Program of the Center for Leadership Development, Inc., is funded by Lilly Endowment in cooperation with Indiana University School of Business.

*   *   *   *   *

424 Union Federal Building
45 N. Pennsylvania Street
Indianapolis, Indiana 46204
(317) 634-9888

1977 CLD Brochure

EXHIBIT K

CENTER FOR LEADERSHIP DEVELOPMENT, IC.

·LEADERSHIP· ·DEVELOPMENT·
CLD
·CENTER·

An experience in

Youth . . .

AWARENESS

*

EXPLORATION

*

OBJECTIVES

- to provide an opportunity for youth to gain familiarity with business

- to acquaint youth with opportunities in business, both from the stand-point of ownership as well as successful career paths

- to acquaint youth with technical areas related to high growth and job opportunities such as various engineering and medical science areas

- to provide opportunities for personal development, including achievement motivation, goal setting and moral value orientation

- to impart an understanding of the free enterprise system -- how it works, competition, and forms of business organization

- to provide an appreciation of business values and individual responsibility to the organization employing him

- to acquaint youth with successful business people, who have made it despite major barriers

- to identify firms which employ youth on a part-time basis while they are still in school, and full-time once they have completed high school or training beyond high school

- to stimulate youth to greater achievement generally through the identification of barriers and how to overcome them

- to acquaint youth with the world of work -- jobs and job requirements, how to get, hold and move up on a job

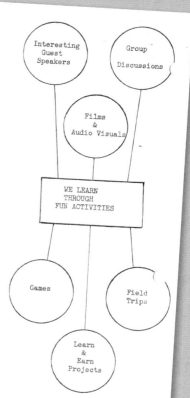

With its president in place, the CLD spent the first half of the year seeking funding for the fledgling operation, securing space in which it could hold classes, and designing the pilot programs that would bring the organization to life. Wentworth and fellow IU professor William Panscher penned the initial grant proposal and request that was submitted to the Lilly Endowment in hopes that it would financially support the new initiative. To the board's delight, the grant was approved with a two-year, $210,000 gift enabling the CLD to move forward.

Eli Lilly and Company was also very generous to the CLD. The pharmaceutical giant provided the CLD with its first home, an A-frame Boy Scout building on the corner of Merrill and New Jersey Streets. With money in the bank and a place in which to hold classes, the CLD board turned its attention to creating course offerings and finding people to participate in them.

"The initial objective as I recall was to offer a series of seminars for high school students in order to help them prepare to go to college and enhance their opportunities," Jim Morris said. "During these seminars, they would work on issues that would help them be successful, such as establishing good study habits and so on. They made visits to college campuses and found out what admission offices were looking for in order to use that information to establish a framework for their program."

From the outset, the CLD had three main goals: to create and implement a process in which to recognize minority leadership, to develop minority talent with an aptitude for entrepreneurship, and to establish a program for high school students who exhibited leadership potential. The latter was the most crucial if the CLD planned to have the organization up and running by the start of the school year, but what kind of program should it be? Bundles felt that students in grades ten to twelve should be the initial target for CLD's youth development program, as these students were on the cusp of making important decisions that could affect the rest of their lives. Bundles said if the CLD could reach out to these young people and give them the opportunity to explore their options, perhaps they would not feel resigned to a substandard fate.

"You've got a heck of a lot of young African American youngsters who do well in the classroom . . . they don't cause [discipline] problems [but] those kids walk out of that classroom and they are neglected. They don't have anyone to talk to about black culture. . . . They don't get that psychological support. The cultural deprivation that goes on in the regular schools—the psychological deprivation—really wipes them out," Bundles said.

Bundles traveled to Philadelphia, Atlanta, and New York to find out what kinds of programs these cities had in place and how they could be adapted to meet the CLD's needs. In order to have the pilot program ready by the fall, they needed to work quickly and reach out to high school guidance counselors so that they could help recruit a wide range of students who had the best chance for success. Straight-A grades were not required for admission into the CLD, but Bundles sought out the high achievers at area high schools in hopes that the organization could help them set goals and learn the steps needed to accomplish them.

"We want the winners among high school students . . . if he or she projects leadership qualities, we are interested," Bundles said. "In order for them to succeed, they must first be motivated. Some will go on to college and some won't [but] we hope that they will continue their educational pursuits."

The Young Adult Advisory Council

Crucial to the CLD's Youth Development Program was the establishment of the Young Adult Advisory Council. The council was an initial group of twenty-five young professional men and women who exhibited the kind of success the CLD hoped their participants might aspire to. They met once a month to brainstorm ideas, develop programs, create marketing materials, schedule guest speakers, and serve as big brothers/big sisters to CLD students. Like the students themselves, the members of the council were diverse. They came from a variety of fields and backgrounds but were all committed to giving minority students an inclusive look into the opportunities available, provided they had the interest and aptitude for them.

Five members of the council agreed to be volunteer "facilitators," or leaders, of the CLD's Youth Development Program. Martha Mitchell of the Indiana Department of Education trained these early facilitators so that they would be able to meet the students' individual needs and draw out the best from them during each session. The CLD hoped that when the students realized these professionals had donated their time and talent for their benefit that it would create long-lasting bonds that would continue for years to come and, hopefully, encourage these students to stay involved with the CLD beyond graduation.

One of the earliest members of the CLD's Young Adult Advisory Council and program facilitators was legendary radio host Amos Brown, a native of Chicago who graduated from Northwestern

BRIEFS

Published by CENTER FOR LEADERSHIP DEVELOPMENT, INC.

Volume 3 - Number 1 — JANUARY - APRIL 1981

A WORD FROM THE EXECUTIVE DIRECTOR S. Henry Bundles, Jr.

It seems such a short time since we wrote a few words at the beginning of 1980 thanking those who continue to support our efforts. Yet time moves on and another year and a fresh beginning are upon us again.

Lilly Endowment, Inc. has awarded the Center for Leadership Development another grant to support our 1981 budget and enable us to continue our efforts for another year.

New friends among student participants, renewed friendships among earlier graduates, and the starting of a new class in the Youth Development Program have come about.

Plans for our Minority Business and Professional Achievers Recognition Awards Dinner on March 2, 1981 have been finalized. Our goal is to eventually make this affair the top program of its kind in central Indiana. With the help of our corporate friends, minority entrepreneurs, advisory council members and all supporters we can accomplish our goal.

Thanks to everyone for assisting the Center for Leadership Development in reaching additional milestones in 1980.

BROWN HEADS DINNER COMMITTEE

Amos Brown III, Assistant General Manager of WTLC radio and a member of the Youth Advisory Council of the Center for Leadership Development is chairman of the first Minority Business and Professional Achievers Recognition Awards Dinner. Mr. Brown submits the following information and invitation:

"We'd like you to join us on Monday evening, March 2, 1981, for a history making event in Indianapolis. It's our first Minority Business and Professional Achievers Recognition Awards Dinner, honoring minority men and women in business and the professions. Plans have been finalized for this evening of recognition, and when you attend, we are sure you will agree this event will have been one long overdue for our community.

With the help of our many corporate friends, minority entrepreneurs, advisory council members and all supporters, we can achieve the goal of making this affair the top dinner program of its kind in Indiana.

Male and female honorees from a substantial number of companies will vie for a total of seven major awards based upon work in their companies and professions and their efforts in making our community a better place in which to live.

The seven major award catagories are:
1. Overall Ideal Achievement (Hayward Campbell Award)
2. Outstanding Woman in Business (Mme C.J. Walker Award)
3. Excellence in Entrepreneurship
4. Achievement in Finance

5. Achievement in Public & Community Service
6. Achievement in Communication
7. Achievement in Professions & Education

As you can tell, these Minority Business and Professional Achievers Recognition Awards will be very much sought after, not only by the minorities in business and the professions, but among area businesses and agencies.

We know you will want to be on hand, on Monday evening, March 2, 1981, in the 500 Ballroom of the Convention Center for this first annual event. Tickets are $20.00 per person and tables are $200.00.

Just contact Barbara Garrett in the CLD office, 634-9888 for more information and registration."

CLD newsletter featuring Amos Brown, longtime Indianapolis radio host

FLOWERS TO . . .

. . . MARY S. WOLFORD

Congratulations to Mary S. Wolford, a member of our Youth Advisory Council who was recently given the 1980 "Networker of the Year" Award. This award is given yearly by the Network of Women in Business.

Mary is a Staff Associate at Indiana Bell Telephone Company and was cited for her leadership in assisting the advancement of women in business and for encouraging the professional growth of career women.

Mary is a graduate of Butler University where she is a graduate student. In addition to being a member of our Youth Advisory Council, she is active in the National Association of Female Executives, the Bell Management Club, Indiana Business Communicators, and a member of the Board of Directors of Big Sisters of Greater Indianapolis. She is listed in the 1981-1982 Who's Who of American Women and was the 1976 "Business Woman of the Year" of the American Business Women's Association New Hope Chapter.

FORMER CLD VOLUNTEER HELPS PLAN NEW DETROIT

It was good to hear from former Youth Advisory Council Member Clintina Cooper Sims who worked very closely with us during the first year of CLD's existence.

Clintina was employed at Chevrolet while here in Indianapolis and was transferred to General Motors (GM) in Detroit. She now works with the GM subsidiary New Center Neighborhood Service Corporation which is a revitalization program to help mid-town Detroit.

Clintina receives our newsletter and was very pleased to know about our continued growth and progress. She also shared a progress report with us on how GM, in conjunction with other business firms and agencies started a multi-million dollar revitalization program in a six block residential area just north of the GM building in Detroit.

The revitalization project will seek to make the New Center area a safe and attractive place to live.

JOBS FOR THE 1980'S

Technical graduates, particulary engineering students, will be in greater demand during the 80's, according to a recent study by the College Placement Council. Science, Math and other technical graduates will also be in greater demand.

BRIEFS
THE CENTER FOR LEADERSHIP DEVELOPMENT

Editors - S. Henry Bundles, Jr.
　　　　　Holbrook Hankinson, Jr.
Circulation - Alicha Anderson, Barbara Garrett

The Briefs is an official publication of the Center for Leadership Development a non-profit organization conceived and funded by Lilly Endowment, Inc., in cooperation with the Indiana University School of Business. Its purpose is to improve the quality and quantity of minorities in business through the development and implementation of training programs. The Briefs is published in September, December, March and June.

CAREER WORKSHOPS HELD

During December, Youth Development Participants who were interested in engineering and medicine along with their parents attended workshops which were designed to increase their awareness of opportunities in these areas.

On December 9th, a "Future Engineers" workshop was conducted at IUPUI's school of Engineering and Technology by Youth Advisory Council Member Dave Hampton, Manager of Engineering at Indiana Bell Telephone Company. The many types of engineering and their differences were discussed. John Hall, director of Purdue University's Minority Engineering Advancement Program (MEAP) was also on hand to discuss career possibilities in engineering.

On December 16th, a workshop for CLD students interested in becoming physicians was conducted at Methodist Hospital. Youth Advisory Council Member Vicky Bailey, Assistant Director of Admissions for the I.U. School of Medicine moderated a distinguished panel of local physicians and medical students who gave their perspective of the medical profession.

Thanks to Dave and Vicky and all those who participated in making our students aware of their opportunities in engineering and medicine.

1981 WINTER/SPRING ACTIVITIES

YOUTH DEVELOPMENT PROGRAM

Parent/Student Orientation	January 4th
Classes Begin	January 10th
Students assigned to	
Youth Advisory Council Members	March 8th
Classes end	April 8th
4th Annual Awards Ceremony	April 24th
Field Trip to I.U. School of Business	April

YOUTH ADVISORY COUNCIL

Council Members assigned to consult with	
Youth Development Program Participants	March 8th

The Youth Advisory Council meets once a month. Prominent Business and Civic Leaders are invited to speak with the group at each meeting.

MINORITY ACHIEVEMENT RECOGNITION

Minority Business and Professional Achievers Recognition Award Dinner	March 2nd

CLD STUDENT RECEIVES BAUSCH & LOMB SCIENCE AWARD

Donald Grant, a participant in CLD's Youth Development Program and a Senior at Arlington High School, was recently awarded the Bausch and Lomb Science Award which includes a medal and a scholarship.

Donald was cited for earning "A's" in every lab science, for his potential in the field of science, and for his outstanding leadership qualities.

Donald says that his participation in CLD has made him a more effective leader in his leadership roles at Arlington. At his high school he is Vice-President of the Senior class, member of the Honor Society, Parliamentarian of the Student Council, Vice-President of the Science Club and Captain of the school's "Brain Game" team.

Donald plans to attend Purdue University and major in engineering.

ACADEMIC OLYMPICS TO PROMOTE "MIND POWER"

The Center for Leadership Development is working with the Indiana Black Expo to sponsor the NAACP's Afro-Academic Cultural Technological Scientific Olympics (ACT-SO).

ACT-SO is a nationwide program to promote academic excellence on a competitive level, through local, state and national competition.

The eligibility requirements to participate are:
1. enrolled in grades 9 through 12
2. a citizen of the United States
3. has never received remuneration for his/her services in their area of competition
4. has developed an expertise in one of the (6) catagories of competition. These catagories are: Performing Arts, Visual Arts, Technical Science, Literary Arts, Applied Science and Social Science.

The local competition is scheduled to be held on February 28 and March 1, 1981 at the St. Peter Claver Center, 3110 N. Sutherland Avenue.

The first place winners in each catagory of competition will receive an all expense paid trip to Denver, Colorado on June 27 and 28, 1981 to compete for the National finals during the NAACP National Convention. There will be other prizes for 1st, 2nd and 3rd place winners.

Deadline for entry is JANUARY 30, 1981.

For further information/applications contact Holbrook Hankinson, Jr., local chairperson at 634-9888 or Charles Williams, state chairperson at 633-6141.

NEWLY FORMED MINORITY BUSINESS ORGANIZATION

The Indianapolis Business Forum is a new organization of minority businesspersons organized to promote minority business enterprise.

Al Green, chief executive officer of Omega Foods, is president of the organization. Other prominent members are CLD Board member Nickey Morris, President of Morris Containers, CLD supporters Lannie Smith, President of L.H. Smith Oil Corporation and Thomas Combs, President of Combs Tool Company.

Several group seminars designed to enhance greater minority business access to corporate purchasing agents are conducted by IBF.

Center for Leadership Development
315 Union Federal Building
45 N. Pennsylvania Street
Indpls., IN 46204

Address correction requested

1981 CLD *Briefs* newsletter

University and moved to Indianapolis in 1975. He secured a position at WTLC Radio as an advertising representative. There he first became acquainted with Bundles and involved with the CLD.

Brown was exactly the type of young, motivated professional the CLD's board of directors wanted their participants to be mentored by. He quickly rose through the ranks of the station to become its manager by 1981 and would go on to become one of the longest serving media managers in the Indianapolis market. He was the on-air host of *Mornings with the Mayor*, which ran from 1977 to 1993, *The*

Bill Mays, founder and owner of the Mays Chemical Company

Bill West, longtime CLD board member

Noon Show, and the long-running *Afternoons with Amos*. He served as the Indianapolis director of strategic research for Radio One, which purchased WTLC in 2001. He was also a featured columnist for the *Indianapolis Recorder* and hosted a television talk show, appropriately titled *The Amos Brown Show*.

Throughout his forty-plus years in broadcasting, Brown was a tireless advocate for the African American community in Indianapolis. He worked with organizations such as the United Negro College Fund, Riley Hospital for Children, Indiana Black Expo, and regularly promoted the efforts of the CLD on air before his death in 2015.

"For nearly forty years, the CLD has helped to educate thousands of African American young men and women who today are in business, are entrepreneurs, and some are parents and grandparents. It's an Indianapolis success story that is in the heart of the 'hood,'" Brown said.

The launch

By the end of the summer, the CLD's pilot programs were planned and its inaugural classes scheduled. IPS educator Holbrook Hankinson designed a forty-hour curriculum based on a course created by a human resource company in Ann Arbor, Michigan, and adapted it to meet the organization's mission. The ten-module course was offered both on

The original members of the CLD's Young Adult Advisory Council

John Baily, president, J. Baily Company

Anthony Barnett, assistant manager, Florsheim Shoes

Michael Barnett, Stuart and Company Investments

Tom Batties, student, Indiana University School of Business

John Brooks, attorney

Amos Brown, assistant manager, WTLC Radio

Lance Bundles, Midwest National Bank

Marilyn Christian, pharmaceutical sales

Robert Collins, law student, Indiana University

Robert Conn, co-owner, Continental Construction

Clintina Cooper, manager, Chevrolet Division of General Motors

Juan Craig, manager, First Federal Savings and Loan

R. David DeFrantz, insurance agent

Doctor Harold Ervin, dentist

Doctor Steven Gordon, physician

Holbrook Hankinson, Indianapolis Public Schools educator

Riley Lloyd, WTLC

Bobbie Lyons, sales, Johnson and Johnson

Nickey Morris, president, Morris Containers, Inc.

Bill Petty, advertising sales, WTLC

Denise Ramsey, director of financial aid, Clark Business College

Yvonne Rawls, administrative assistant, Indiana Department of Corrections

Mr. and Mrs. Lodia Richards, Chevrolet Division of General Motors

Ben Singletary, student, Indiana University School of Business

Perry Washington, engineer, Delco Remy

Saturday mornings and on specific weeknights, depending on a student's extracurricular schedule. It would help tenth to twelfth graders look inside themselves to identify their strengths, needs, and goals; to determine their values; and explore their particular areas of interest.

On October 18, 1977, Bundles and the CLD board held a press conference with members of the local media to announce the new initiative and outline the offerings to the public. Bundles told the assembly that the CLD had extended invitations to forty-two students for the fall semester of classes, which included an even number of young men and women. He hoped that after taking part in the CLD's youth development program, these students would feel that they were destined for greatness, rather than set up for failure.

"We want to inform minorities of potential career opportunities, give them an understanding of the free enterprise system, to develop leadership qualities and have a better understanding of business and the American marketplace," Bundles said.

But first, those students had to discover who they were inside.

ARTICLES OF INCORPORATION

OF

CENTER FOR LEADERSHIP DEVELOPMENT, INC.

The undersigned incorporator, desiring to form a corporation (hereafter referred to as the "Corporation") pursuant to the provisions of the Indiana Not-for-Profit Corporation Act of 1971 (hereafter referred to as the "Act"), hereby executes the following Articles of Incorporation:

ARTICLE I

Name

The name of the Corporation is Center for Leadership Development, Inc.

ARTICLE II

Purposes

The Corporation is organized exclusively for the purposes of carrying out the educational and charitable purposes of, and performing the educational and charitable functions of, Indiana University and the Indiana University School of Business.

In furtherance of such purposes, the Corporation shall serve and assist Indiana University and the Indiana University School of Business in aiding and encouraging the entry and advancement of members of racial minorities in leadership and management positions in business and industry.

Articles of Incorporation

EXHIBIT A

Department of the Treasury

District Director
Internal Revenue Service
Date: MAR 03 1977 | In reply refer to:
L-178 FPEO:WOM.Ag

CIN: EO: '77 0 4 1 1

Center for Leadership Development, Inc.
1300 West Michigan Street
Indianapolis, Indiana 46202

Gentlemen:

Based on information supplied, and assuming your operations will be as stated in your application for recognition of exemption, we have determined you are exempt from Federal income tax under section 501(c)(3) of the Internal Revenue Code.

We have further determined you are not a private foundation within the meaning of section 509(a) of the Code, because you are an organization described in section 509(a)(3).

You are not liable for social security (FICA) taxes unless you file a waiver of exemption certificate as provided in the Federal Insurance Contributions Act. You are not liable for the taxes imposed under the Federal Unemployment Tax Act (FUTA).

Since you are not a private foundation, you are not subject to the excise taxes under Chapter 42 of the Code. However, you are not automatically exempt from other Federal excise taxes. If you have any questions about excise, employment, or other Federal taxes, please let us know.

Donors may deduct contributions to you as provided in section 170 of the Code. Bequests, legacies, devises, transfers, or gifts to you or for your use are deductible for Federal estate and gift tax purposes if they meet the applicable provisions of sections 2055, 2106, and 2522 of the Code.

If your purposes, character, or method of operation is changed, please let us know so we can consider the effect of the change on your exempt status. Also, you should inform us of all changes in your name or address.

(Over)

Form L-178 (Rev. 8-73)

IRS Determination Letter

STATE OF INDIANA
OFFICE OF THE SECRETARY OF STATE

To Whom These Presents Come, Greeting:

CERTIFICATE OF INCORPORATION

CENTER FOR LEADERSHIP DEVELOPMENT, INC.

I, LARRY A. CONRAD, Secretary of State of the State of Indiana, hereby certify that Articles of Incorporation of the above not-for-profit corporation, in the form prescribed by this Office, prepared and signed in duplicate by the Incorporator(s) and acknowledged and verified by the same before a Notary Public, have been presented to me at this office accompanied by the fees prescribed by law; that I have found such Articles conform to law; that I have endorsed my approval upon the duplicate copies of such Articles; that all fees have been paid as required by law; that one copy of such Articles has been filed in this office; and that the remaining copy(ies) of such Articles bearing the endorsement of my approval and filing has (have) been returned by me to the incorporator(s) or his (their) representatives; all as prescribed by the Indiana Not-For-Profit Corporation Act of 1971.

NOW, THEREFORE, I hereby issue to such Corporation this Certificate of Incorporation, and further certify that its corporate existance has begun.

In Witness Whereof, I have hereunto set my hand and affixed the seal of the State of Indiana, at the City of Indianapolis, this _____3rd_____ *day of* January _____ 19 77

LARRY A. CONRAD, *Secretary of State*

By _____ *Deputy*

Certificate of Incorporation

Chapter 3 Self-Discovery/Career Exploration Project

Before they can become the next generation of community leaders, minority youth have to be given the tools they need in order to succeed. Over the years, the Center for Leadership Development implemented a number of initiatives to do just that, but the effort that emerged from the initial Youth Development Program was Self-Discovery/Career Exploration Project.

Written by Holbrook Hankinson, an educator at Broad Ripple High School and a member of the CLD's Young Adult Advisory Council, the Self-Discovery/Career Exploration Project was launched in September 1977 and was designed to help students answer three fundamental questions:

- Who am I?
- Where am I going?
- How will I get there?

In order to help participants answer these questions, facilitators led classes on a wide variety of topics that would help students get to know themselves in a way they had not before. The sessions emphasized key areas that teachers and guidance counselors may not have covered. It was believed that if students were given the opportunity to look within themselves, they would gain greater insight into their personal, emotional, and professional aspirations. This insight would help teens set goals, make effective decisions about their future plans, and prepare for any obstacles that might stand in the way of their achievement.

When Hankinson agreed to write the curriculum for the Self-Discovery/Career Exploration Project, he was unsure what elements should be included. As a teacher, he knew a number of minorities were dropping out or leaving high school without the life skills they needed to thrive at the post-secondary

Steven L. Jones, CLD alumni ('81)

Steve Jones Recalls Holbrook Hankinson's impact

When it comes to facilitators who made a big impact on the lives of early CLD students, Holbrook Hankinson is a name that comes up time and time again. For students such as Steve Jones (CLD '81), Hankinson was the perfect example of what a successful minority male could be.

"You couldn't go through CLD and not know Holbrook," Jones said. "The boys looked up to him. The girls just loved him, and he really had a kind of following."

Jones said Hankinson gave CLD students the wisdom and insight as to what businesses and organizations were looking for in their employees and how they could plant the seeds for future success.

"More than anything else, he opened my eyes and expanded my horizons," he said.

level, but he also knew that lecturing them was not the most effective way in which to get a message across. The sessions had to be interactive and something the students could relate to. "You have to develop something that adapts to the way kids want to learn," he said. "Schools don't always do a good job of that."

Hankinson said Henry Bundles brought in human resource professionals from area businesses to discuss their experiences with young people. In those forums Hankinson learned about the key deficiencies preventing students from getting ahead. Most of them did not know how to make a good first impression, look an interviewer in the eye,

or conduct themselves in a professional manner. Hankinson determined that this lack of polish was not only due to a deficiency in education, but also a lack of self-awareness.

That became the foundation for the program: to give students the skills they would need in order to get ahead in life. Although most of the students came from two-parent, middle-class families, there was a lot they did not understand in terms of how the business world worked. They had to learn how to dress for success, make a good first impression, network with others, and put their best foot forward in professional settings. Hankinson said that was not something they could learn sitting behind

CLD "In Time, On Time, Everytime" motto

Holbrook Hankinson, early CLD facilitator

a desk or could demonstrate unless they believed they had potential inside of them. "That's where I came in," he said. "I made a point of helping them see that light inside of them and telling them that I saw it too."

Life Lessons

One of the first lessons every student learned when they enrolled in the Self-Discovery/Career Exploration Project was the unofficial motto of the CLD: "In time, on time, every time, except when a little ahead of time and that's better time." It is an expression Bundles created to impress upon CLD students the importance of being prompt in everything they did. It is a message that hit home with students such as Kim Lawrence-Curry (CLD '79), who said although she loved coming to the CLD sessions, meeting other high school students from the city, and working with someone as smart and

engaged as Hankinson, it was the "In time" saying that stuck with her the most. "I live by the 'In time' slogan daily," she said.

In order to answer the first question, "Who am I?," students were led through a variety of exercises designed to help them identify their personal strengths, weaknesses, values, needs, personality type, and lifestyle. They also worked to develop better communication skills—something Bundles believed was central to a student's future success.

Throughout his extensive career, Bundles spent a lot of time evaluating people, and he saw how their ability to communicate could make or break their chances in business. No matter if someone was navigating a network event, making that all-important first presentation, working in a group setting, or fielding questions in an interview, he knew that communication skills were paramount to the process. Bundles believed it was important to encourage young people to improve the way they wrote and spoke to others in order to be taken seriously and to avoid the use of Ebonics whenever possible.

"If you expect to be taken seriously in the United States of America, it is absolutely essential that you express yourself in an articulate manner," he said. "There are some black educators who would have you believe that so-called 'Black English' is acceptable and should not hinder your professional progress. Let me dispel that myth. There is no Black English. There is only Standard English. Black English is not acceptable. The only things it will get you are wages that are not commensurate with your education and expectations plus a lifetime of

The original Self-Discovery/Career Exploration Project was a forty-hour series of courses held in two formats (weeknights or weekends) in order to best meet the needs of the students involved. The original outline of the program included ten sections that focused on the following objectives:

1. **Self-exploration:** Exploring one's interests and strengths.

2. **Exploring your needs:** Understanding one's personality and lifestyle.

3. **Self-directed search:** Applying self-understanding to career options.

4. **Self-directed search:** Determining and sharing your values (including those in conflict with society).

5. **Goal setting:** Making goals, setting them, and creating a road map to achieve them.

6. **Field Trip:** Small-group job shadow opportunity at an area business.

7. **Overcoming barriers:** Identifying them, coping with them, and moving beyond them.

8. **Using information:** How to find out what you need to know, what to do with that information once you have it, enhancing relationships, and listening to feedback.

9. **Creating your future:** Streamlining your options, projecting the possibilities, developing a blueprint for your life, and creating a future version of one's self.

10. **Final session:** Re-respond to the three initial questions again: Who am I? Where am I going? How will I get there?

wondering why you cannot succeed in your chosen field."

Bundles also knew that when young people are undecided about the direction of their life it is usually because they have limited knowledge of the options available to them. When they see the possibilities and have some idea of where they want to be in a few years, they can begin to unravel the mystery of how they will get there. The Self-Discovery/Career Exploration Project allows students to make a connection between a good education and a good career, develop the skills and behaviors necessary to find future employment, and have an idea of the kinds of fields they may be best suited for.

A Recipe for Success

Students who participated in the first semester of CLD programming represented a wide range of area high schools, including Arlington, Arsenal Tech, Bishop Chatard, Brebeuf Jesuit, Broad Ripple, North Central, Shortridge, and Washington, and right from the start it was obvious that the CLD was destined for success. "It taught me some valuable lessons about how to prepare for college and create solid study skills that would help me in the future," said Lawrence-Curry.

Wendell Ray (CLD '82) was typical of the kind of student who benefited from the CLD's pilot program. As a child he longed to be a football player

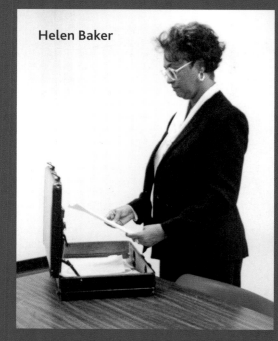
Helen Baker

1987 Business Orientation facilitators and students

Helen Baker's Contributions to the CLD

Doctor Jacqueline Greenwood, a CLD board member and former principal at Arlington High School, said Baker not only helped write much of the CLD's curriculum but also was instrumental in reaching out to area schools to get their support for the organization.

"Helen Baker believed in the CLD's mission right from the start and was able to make those connections with schools, like Arlington, that encouraged teachers, guidance counselors and administrators to recommend students to the program," she said. "Helen Baker, Henry Bundles, and others got the schools on board so that they could help students see beyond what is to what could be."

INDIANA UNIVERSITY and the Center for Leadership Development (CLD) recently held graduation exercises for students participating in its Business Orientation Project (B.O.P.). Some of the students who received certificates of completion are shown above with Hassan Danesh (front row left), representing Indiana University, and Henry Crews (second row left), who facilitated the class for CLD. Students on the front row are Tracee Tate, Machelle Smith, Shanell Crockett and Malcolm Thompson. On second row are Kelly Butler, Chris Elliott, Adrienne Woodard and Kara Endsley. Jason Smith is pictured rear.

Newspaper article featuring 1987 Business Orientation Project participants

but did not grow big enough to achieve gridiron greatness. He then decided to be an architect, and then an attorney, but it was not until he took a broadcasting class at Broad Ripple High School that he considered a career in radio. Like a lot of young people who go through life with a number of big dreams, he had no idea how to fulfill them. Luckily, the CLD's youth development program was there to help with the process.

Ray said the Self-Discovery/Career Exploration Project allowed him to get his life on track by showing him how to prepare for the road ahead. After graduating from high school in 1982, he attended Indiana Wesleyan University and began working at WTLC Radio. His résumé also included a stint at WFYI Channel 20 before he became the manager of community affairs for the CLD. Today, he is the director of education for the Illinois Media School in Chicago and has been named a distinguished alum of his high school alma mater.

Ray said students who take part in the CLD's Self-Discovery/Career Exploration Project came out of it with a better understanding of themselves and what it takes to turn their dreams into realities. "That student . . . may all of a sudden understand, 'Hey, I can be somebody. I can achieve and I too can become a leader in my school.' It builds self-esteem," he said.

Of course, Ray was not the only early CLD participant who felt that the project made a difference in their lives. Bonita Neal (CLD '80) said the Self-Discovery/Career Exploration Project helped propel her to become the first college graduate in her family. Neal attended Washington High School in the late 1970s when few African American students aspired to attend college. She said the CLD not only helped her understand how important higher education could be but also introduced her to professionals who talked the talk and walked the walk. Today, as a guidance counselor for Belzer Middle School in Lawrence Township, she pays it forward to the kids she comes in contact with on a daily basis.

"To have someone come into my life and talk about opportunities and the things you can do—having a job, making decent money—that was a great experience for me and I needed it at the time. . . . Back then, it was like a hope," she said.

Helen Baker with CLD facilitators, including President Dennis Bland

Henry Bundles (center) with Helen Baker, A'Lelia Bundles, and CLD alumni and staff. Amos Brown is at the far left.

The Woman behind the Lessons

In addition to Bundles and Hankinson, there was another person who was central to the overall success of the CLD: Helen Baker, the woman behind the lessons that transformed students' lives.

Baker was an educator who served as a fourth-grade teacher at White River School, as well as a special reading teacher at John Strange Elementary School before going on to become the assistant principal (and later principal) at Greenbriar Elementary School in Washington Township. She began as a volunteer with the CLD in 1978 but became a full-time employee ten years later, serving as the vice president of administration/curriculum until her retirement in 2000. Although she is quick to point out that many helped with the CLD program planning, she is proud of the work she accomplished with the organization, which stood for everything she believed in.

"It provides an oasis for minority children, mostly African American," she said. "The Center provides youth a place where they don't feel discriminated against."

As the students responded to the Self-Discovery/Career Exploration Project, their teachers and administrators began to feel the impact as well. At Arlington High School, Principal Jackie Greenwood liked the way the CLD took lessons from the classroom, applied them to real-life situations, and got the students around other like-minded, goal-oriented people. She was so impressed with the program that whenever she saw potential in a child, she tried to get them involved with the CLD right away.

Students and facilitators Role Model Mentor Program, 1987

"It just enhances what we do at the academic level," she said. "When a child goes through the CLD, they wear the Self-Discovery/Career Exploration Project like a badge of honor. They are proud to be a part of it and that's how you change the culture, by giving children a sense of pride and reinforcing the lessons they are learning in the classroom."

Parents also liked what they saw when their child participated in the CLD program, with many seeing an increase in focus and development of concrete goals long after the Self-Discovery/Career Exploration Project was over. Marvis Fulford said the CLD provided a valuable, meaningful, and worthwhile service to her child that was also supportive of parents. "I imagine that all parents would want their children to excel and to succeed," said Fulford, "and I think this program helps them do that."

Even businesses realized the important work the CLD was doing through its Youth Development Program and how their efforts were producing highly motivated, achievement-oriented individuals who make better employees. Eric W. Vetter, the vice president of management and organizational development for the Boehringer Mannheim Group, said, "I believe it is the finest youth group program in the U.S. There is nothing else like it."

"In time, on time except when a little ahead of time and that's better time."

Early CLD students

The First CLD Graduates

Although only eight high schools participated during that first semester of CLD programming, as word got out about the new initiative more schools were eager to join. New sessions were added in the spring of 1978, and all of the students who completed the program were recognized with a certificate at the CLD's inaugural awards ceremony on March 28, 1978.

SEPTEMBER-FEBRUARY CLASS

Troy Adams	George Harrison III	Sherri Bryant	Anitra Parrish
Brian Akers	Keith Hayes	Theresa Bunch	Felice Polin
Frank Alexander	Aubrey Hubbard	Wanda Bunch	Daren Pope
Alicha Anderson	Jeffery Johnson	Emmitt Carlton	Gwen Richards
Cynthia M. Anderson	Felicia Kirkman	Alicia Currin	Velvet Richardson
Lisa Austin	Stacy Lawrence	Vincent Dodson	Annette Robinson
Letita Bedgett	Michelle Lewis	Billy Evans	Morris Smith
Grace Bates	Darlene Matthews	Karen Evans	Rochelle Webster
Thelma Boyd	Linda McFarland	Steven Fernandez	Rosiland Wells
Monica Bradford	Rita Montgomery	Andre Ford	Clarence Wilson
Linda Brownlow	Lawrence Morgan	John Glass III	

JANUARY-APRIL CLASS

Tresanay Amos	Gale Lolla	Kathy Ferguson	Jeanette Preston
Cynthia A. Anderson	Nan'Arlisa Major	Linda Floyd	Derek Pullins
David Anderson	Starla Mathews	Patricia Gardener	Mary Ramsey
Teresa Anderson	Angela McKoy	Rochelle Gilbert	Tonya Reeves
Charles Benberry	Orlando Miller	Donald Grant	Kimberly Ridley
Geowanda Britton	Craig Morris	Carolle Griffin	Diane Robinson
Katherine Brooks	Frank Myers	Kevin Hampton	Maria Robinson
Wayne Clark	Mary Jo Newborn	Vincent Harper	Cynthia Sherrod
David Clemmons	Franklyn Ogelvie	Bonita Harrington	Portia Sholar
Christina Colvin	Vickie Outlaw	Barbara Howard	Laverne Spencer
Marier Cox	Karen Owen	Bobby Hubbard	Wyquetta Terri
Allison Craig	Traci Page	Pamela Humbles	Rhoda Thomas
Jeffrey Crews	Darlene Parks	Jill Jackson	Terri Tooley
Kevin Dailey	Justina Parson	Tinya Jackson	Michelle Walker
William Dailey	Priscella Perkins	Robyn Lee	Robert Welch
Bianca Embry	Sharon Pitts	Lorenzo Lewis	Kanvass White
Elaine Evans	Mary Pounds		

> "Everyone wants minority students to succeed. CLD creates success stories."
>
> *Jerry Semler*

Chapter 4 Building Bonds, Acknowledging Achievement

With its youth development program successfully under way, the Center for Leadership Development turned its attention to its other goals, namely, the desire to spread awareness about the organization throughout central Indiana, to garner the support of the local business community, to support minority professionals, and to celebrate their accomplishments in an annual event designed to highlight achievers.

A Network of Friends

Henry Bundles understood that it takes a village to raise a child and that people tend to support those entities that they help create. That is why he felt it was important for the CLD to develop a symbiotic relationship with local businesses throughout the city. In July 1978 he organized a corporate luncheon in downtown Indianapolis to introduce business leaders to the CLD, showcase its first two semesters, and invite prominent area leaders to become involved. The CLD not only needed the financial support of these firms, but it also needed a network of friends who could provide the organization with additional resources, volunteers, and employment opportunities for CLD graduates.

As Bundles outlined the CLD's vision, he pointed out how the organization differed from Junior Achievement and other business-preparedness programs by striving to develop the whole person with an emphasis on leadership, group guidance, meaningful values, and career exploration. "Despite its initial success, the Center for Leadership Development is convinced that a great deal of its support must come from the private business sector," he said in his remarks at the luncheon. "As we try to make goals relevant, practical in terms of today's business world, we realize that such goals cannot be reached without strong ties to the business community."

There were twenty-seven people at the luncheon, and after listening to Bundles a number of them pledged their support through financial contributions, volunteers, and a number of guest speakers who would attend CLD sessions to talk about their careers. Some of them even joined the CLD's Young

Early supporters of the CLD's Youth Development program included:

- **Eli Lilly and Company**
- **Lilly Endowment**
- **Indiana University School of Business**
- **A&P Food Stores**
- **American Fletcher National Bank**
- **American States Insurance**
- **William H. Block Company**
- **Dow Chemical Company**
- **IBM Corporation**
- **Indiana National Bank**
- **Indiana Bell Telephone Company**
- **L. S. Ayres and Company**
- **Mayflower Corporation**
- **Morris Plan**
- **Peat, Marwick and Mitchell Accounting Firm**
- **WTTV Channel 4**
- **International Harvester**
- **Gene Glick Company**

Adult Advisory Council and allowed students to shadow them as they went about their day-to-day activities. Some of those early guest speakers would go on to become prominent names throughout the Indianapolis community and role models for an entire generation of up-and-coming leaders. They included:

Community leader Moses Gray

Jerry Semler, former CLD board chair

- Julia Carson, state senator and former employee of Cummins Engineering
- Clarice Banks, freelance fashion illustrator for William H. Block and L. S. Ayres and Company department stores
- Doctor Arthur Sumrall, dermatologist
- Payton Wells, owner, Payton Wells Auto Agency
- Joseph Slash, deputy mayor, City of Indianapolis

Tony Lamont said he still remembers when Bundles first asked him to be a guest speaker for the Self-Discovery/Career Exploration Project in the late 1980s. As a local radio personality with WTLC 106.7 FM, Lamont told the students about his career in broadcasting and shared a little of his back story. He grew up in a single-parent household where he had big dreams of succeeding in life. The odds were stacked against him, and there were trials and tribulations along the way. But with hard work, dedication, and perseverance he was able to turn his dreams into a reality. If he could do it, so could they; provided that they had the right work ethic and the tools they were gaining through the CLD.

"The CLD program enables people throughout the central Indiana area to come in and encourage kids in a way I've never seen before," said Lamont. "It takes them at face value, acknowledges where they are in life, commiserates with their unique situation and gives them the tools they need to grow into themselves and get where they want to be in the future."

Lamont said in the years that he had been affiliated with the CLD, he felt the organization gave the kids a sense of pride, taught them to be selfless

members of the community in which they would live and work, and exposed them to real role models they could look up to. "These role models and guest speakers paint a broader picture for these kids which helps them see that no matter what difficulties they face, those difficulties are only part of the journey. They do not determine their destination," he said.

Annual Breakfast Meeting

In addition to providing students with guest speakers and role models during their program sessions, the CLD also enabled its students to meet with and speak to members of the minority business and professional community through the annual breakfast meeting. Held in July, the Minority Business/ CLD Student Breakfast Meeting was created to expose students to local business professionals and give them the chance to practice their networking skills.

Owners of leading Indianapolis-based minority businesses sponsored the event and in many cases supplied tables with representatives who engaged students in conversation, learned more about them, and led the tables in group discussions that focused on a wide range of career-related topics such as: "Dressing and grooming for a job interview," "The declining enrollment of minorities in college," "Do's and don'ts of the interviewing process," and "Is community involvement really important?" These topics and responses were later shared with the larger group so that all attendees benefited from the knowledge that was shared.

Liz Daily, pictured with her husband, George Crawford, receives CLD award

The CLD believed that the conversations that occurred during these breakfast meetings offered students the motivation to enter into careers that would aid in improving the quality and quantity of minority talent in business and industry. Many valuable job and career contacts were gained by the students who attended these events, and businesses were able to see some of the minority talent the CLD was producing through its programming.

Semler Steps Up

Key to the CLD's success was the ability of Bundles to convince many of the city's most influential men and women to see the need for the program and support its mission early on. Bundles was grounded in the Indianapolis community, and he had an extensive network of friends and business associates. When he needed their help he did not hesitate to ask. "That's how we got Schulyer Otteson, Tom King, Eldon Campbell, and Jerry Semler on board," said Bill West, former president and CEO of Mays Chemical Company and CLD board member since 1989.

Semler's contributions to the CLD cannot be overstated. As the president of American United Life (today, OneAmerica) he knew Bundles through the 500 Festival Association, where they both sat

Congresswoman Julia Carson and Henry Bundles

Joe Slash, former CLD board member

Henry Bundles and former Indianapolis mayor Steve Goldsmith

Accomplished Achievement Award and Madame C. J. Walker Award

The top honors given each year at the Minority Achiever Awards are the Accomplished Achievement Award and the Madame C. J. Walker Award. Originally named for Doctor Haywood Campbell, a man who represented achievement in every aspect of business, industry, and the professions, the Accomplished Achiever Award is presented to a minority male who has followed in Campbell's footsteps and is motivated to succeed in everything they do. The Madame C.J. Walker Award, named for hair care entrepreneur Madame C. J. Walker, is bestowed upon a minority woman who represents achievement in the area of business. The following people have been the recipients of these two overall categories over the years.

Accomplished Achievement Award

1981: W. T. Ray

1982: Judge Webster Brewer

1983: Doctor Joseph Taylor

1984: Doctor George Rawls

1985: Doctor Frank Lloyd

1986: Joseph Slash

1987: Joseph Kimbrew

1988: Raymon Wilson

1989: Doctor Lehman Adams

1990: Robert Taylor

1991: Leroy Woodard

1992: Michael Wright

1993: Robert Wood

1994: Samuel Johnson

1995: Richard Bonds

1996: Byron Mason

1997: James Daughtry

1998: Billy Knight

1999: Ben Carter

2000: Lloyd Lyons

2001: Doctor John Joyner

2002: Doctor Eugene G. White

2003: Sam H. Jones

2004: Doctor Everette Freeman, Ed.D

2005: Doctor Clark J. Simons

2006: Samuel L. Odle

2007: Doctor Charlie Nelms

2008: Doctor Bobby Fong

2009: Ron Hunter

2010: Marvin L. White

2011: William G. Mays

2012: Bishop T. Garrott Benjamin Jr.

2013: The Honorable William (Bill) Crawford

2014: Pastor Jeffrey A. Johnson, Sr.

2015: Max Siegel

2016: Roy Smith

2017: Derrick Burks

Madame C. J. Walker Award

1981: Jean Smith

1982: Mamie Townsend

1983: Katherine Bailey

1984: Patricia Turner-Smith

1985: Dorothy Jones

1986: Osma Spurlock

1987: Leslie Anderson- Hollingsworth

1988: Mary Harden

1989: Pat Browne

1990: Paula Parker-Sawyers

1991: Judith Waugh

1992: Doctor Jacqueline Greenwood

1993: Alecia DeCoudreaux

1994: Fay Williams

1995: Robbie Williams

1996: Lillian Stokes

1997: Marsha Oliver

1998: Earline Moore

1999: Jarnell Burks Craig

2000: Doctor Lyvonne Washington

2001: Vicky Bailey

2002: Helen E. Baker Bundles

2003: Carolyn M. Coleman

2004: Alpha Blackburn

2005: Patzetta Trice

2006: Yvonne Perkins

2007: Sheriee Ladd

2008: Doctor Khaula Murtadha

2009: Andrea Neely

2010: Deborah Oatts

2011: The Honorable Tanya Walton Pratt

2012: Mari Evans

2013: Tamika Catchings

2014: Myra Selby

2015: Doctor Virginia Caine

2016: Thea Kelly

2017: Betty Perry

on the board, and when Bundles called to request a meeting, Semler readily set up the appointment. "Henry was so afraid I would say no that he brought Indianapolis Chamber president Carl Dortch along for reinforcement," Semler recalled. "He didn't have to do that. I knew Henry. I was impressed with his passion to help minority kids go to college, and I wanted to help him."

And help him he did. West said Semler's support helped legitimize the CLD and insure that it would be a well-regarded institution. He could authorize large donations without asking anyone else, and he was able to help propel the program to the next level. West said even if people knew nothing about the CLD or who Bundles was, when they heard that Semler was the chairman of the board they knew the CLD must be doing something right. "When Jerry reached out to potential donors, people took his call. They were honored to help him, and he was the person who helped turn the Minority Achievers Dinner into the premiere event it is today," West said.

Minority Achievers

Since its inception in 1977, the CLD believed it was important to identify and recognize exceptional minority talent. The organization knew that throughout central Indiana there were exceptional men and women working diligently to make their communities a better place in which to live. These individuals participated in a wide range of activities. They volunteered their time and effort to a variety of initiatives, and they achieved personal excellence in their chosen fields. They were important citizens

Local radio personality Tony Lamont speaking at student luncheon

Thomas King, CLD board chair

who deserved to have their accomplishments acknowledged. In 1981 the CLD decided to do just that by creating the Minority Business and Professional Achievers Recognition Awards Dinner.

The purpose of the awards dinner (now known as the Minority Achiever Awards and Scholarship Gala) was to honor those individuals who made significant contributions to their place of employment or who performed outstanding service for the betterment of their community. The CLD takes pride in showcasing these individuals in an event that not only highlights their individual contributions but also encourages others to reach similar levels of achievement.

"Henry Bundles and the CLD Board were very committed to the idea of recognizing those people who were already in the business community and advancing their efforts. Through the Minority Achievers Recognition Dinner they were able to do just that and it made the local companies and organizations sit up and take notice of the minority talent they had," said Holbrook Hankinson.

Originally, the Minority Achievers Awards Dinner was designed to be a celebratory event and nothing more, but Eldon Campbell felt it could be an opportunity to raise funds and spread the word about the CLD opportunity. Semler agreed and wrote the first sponsorship check. "Jerry believed we should have title sponsors, sell tickets, and allow businesses to sponsor tables, and that was very important," West said. "We had the long-term commitment from Lilly, but there was an understanding that we were to raise our own funds as well, and this was a great way to do it."

The first Minority Business and Professional Achievers Recognition Awards Dinner was held on Monday, March 2, 1981, at the Indiana Convention Center 500 Ballroom. The master of ceremonies for the event was Amos Brown, and Reverend Andrew Brown, pastor of Saint John Missionary Baptist Church, presented the invocation. More than 130 men and women representing sixty-seven firms were nominated for their work with the top two honors going to W. T. Ray, executive assistant to former Governor Otis Bowen, and Jean Smith, vice president of public relations at Indiana National Bank.

In 1988 two of the nominees for the Minority Business and Professional Achievers Awards were CLD alums. This led to the organization creating the "Up and Coming" achiever award in 1990 for professionals under the age of thirty. Naturally, many of those who were given this award were and continue to be graduates of the CLD Self-Discovery/Career Exploration Project and this led to the establishment of the CLD Alumni Association Distinguished

Richard Bonds and Robbie Williams, Minority Achievers Awards recipients

Presenters Jerry Harness, David Mayes, and award recipient

Alumni Award as well. Although there were originally eleven award categories for the event, by 1990 it had swelled to thirteen. Today, there are fifteen and include the following categories:

- Achievement in Arts and Entertainment*
- Achievement in Business and Industry*
- Achievement in Communication/PR/ Advertising*
- Achievement in Education (K-12)*
- Achievement in Education (Post-secondary)
- Achievement in Entrepreneurship*
- Achievement in Financial Services*
- Achievement in Professions*
- Achievement in Public and Community Service*
- Achievement in Science and Technical Disciplines
- "Up and Coming" Achiever
- Human Achievement

Early Minority Achievers Awards recipients

Board Award recipients

William Mays, John Thompson, and Bill West

Annual Corporate Luncheon Program

- Distinguished CLD Alumni Award
- S. Henry Bundles Jr. Award for Service to the Center for Leadership Development

(*Denotes one of the original award categories)

Today, the Minority Achievers Awards and Scholarship Gala is one of the city's premiere events, and for those who take part in the celebration it has a lasting impact on their lives—no matter if they are an honoree, a CLD student host/presenter, or a community leader watching his or her employee or associate soar to new heights. Semler said the

event has grown beyond his expectations and is no longer a night in which only local business people are recognized. It is also an event where people see the next generation of minority leaders take their first steps into a larger arena. "Each year the CLD raises about $3 million in scholarships for its students from colleges and universities which are presented that night," he said. "It is just incredible. Every employer wants good minority talent, and thanks to the CLD and these scholarships that talent has the opportunity to succeed," he said.

Current CLD board of directors chairman Thomas A. King said that it has been his privilege to be part of the CLD since its beginning, and each year his heart fills with pride as he meets the latest class of honorees, many of whom benefited from CLD programming when they were younger. "It is only fitting that these individuals be recognized by the CLD," said King. "And it is only fitting that they be lifted up to current CLD participants as role models."

> "None of us even thought about how far the program would develop."
>
> *Henry Bundles*

Chapter 5 Growing with the Times

When the Center for Leadership Development launched its youth development program in 1977 and held its first Self-Discovery/Career Exploration Project class, Henry Bundles hoped that there would come a time when the organization would work itself out of existence. He longed for the day when the CLD would be so successful minority youth would no longer need a program geared for their specific needs. He turned out to be half right. The CLD was very successful, but the more successful it was, the more the community came to rely on it.

Holbrook Hankinson, a former facilitator with the Self-Discovery/Career Exploration Project and assistant director of the organization, said he is not surprised that the CLD has lasted forty years. "It's a great program, but in a way, it's sad that it still exists," he said. "However, when schools do not make the necessary changes or adapt themselves to the way in which kids learn and respond to their lessons, it makes CLD's programming more important than ever."

It also meant that the organization's programs had to evolve, adapt, and move with the times in order to meet the needs of the current generation. Luckily the CLD staff and board of directors were willing to do just that so that they could avoid stagnation and remain relevant in a changing world.

Expanding the program

After the early success of its first two semesters, the CLD created an advanced program that would take place over the summer. Designed by Hankinson and facilitated by Robert Steele, the summer program was geared to help current high school and college-bound students find summer employment. The six-week program was held at Indiana University–Purdue University at Indianapolis and covered such topics as résumé writing, filling out a job application, making a good professional impression, understanding basic financial transactions, and connecting students with potential employers.

Early students with Helen Baker and Henry Bundles

Once those summer sessions were over, it was obvious that these skills were a critical component of a student's overall success, so the program organizers decided to revamp the Self-Discovery/Career Exploration Project to include some of these elements. The new format would last thirteen weeks and included modules on:

- Communication and success
- Effective presentation skills
- Working together
- How to pay for college
- Assertiveness training
- Making good decisions

- Setting career goals
- Effective study and time-management skills
- Examining barriers
- Dressing for success
- Effective interviewing skills
- Career goal presentations
- Final exercise—putting it all together.

After spending thirteen weeks identifying career paths that might be right for them and preparing for the road ahead, the CLD wanted students to have the chance to get up close and personal with those areas of interest in order to see what it took to be successful in those fields. To do so, the CLD organized job shadow opportunities with facilitators and members of the Young Adult Advisory Council. (Today, this program is known as the Role Model/Advisor Experience.)

Some matchups were easier than others, but CLD facilitators and Young Adult Advisory Council members were not the kind of people to give up when the going got tough. Throughout the CLD's forty-year history, there have been a number of volunteers who have gone above and beyond to give their students a proper job-shadow experience. However, one individual stands out: Sandy Tompkins who, in 1980, was a human resources professional at Indiana Bell.

Tomkins was charged with locating a shadow opportunity for Alicia Fleming (CLD '81), who hoped to attend college and become a French and Spanish interpreter. Although she had some contacts in fields where people used language in their careers, there were not a lot of language translators in the Indianapolis area and Tompkins was not having any luck making a professional connection for the girl. After exhausting her contacts, Tomkins made one last-ditch attempt. She called the director of the Immigration and Naturalization Service office in Chicago and arranged for Fleming to sit in on a court hearing involving an English-speaking judge, Spanish-speaking immigrants, and their interpreter, who kept the conversation flowing. The experience confirmed Fleming's career choice, and after speaking to the interpreter she returned to Indianapolis and immediately began looking for ways in which she could improve her language skills in a volunteer capacity. "[Sandy's] commitment meant everything to me," Fleming said. "She was

Doctor Anthony Mimms as a young CLD student

highly intelligent and had a similar love for languages as I did. We were also similar in our tenacity and the ability to go after our goals."

Fleming said she already knew what career path she wanted to pursue before joining the CLD, but she was thrilled to have a mentor in Tomkins, who taught her a lot about professionalism and how to be a tenacious businesswoman. In 2017 Fleming was an associate instructor of Spanish and Latino studies at IUPUI and the author of a poetry collection titled *My Soul Inside Out*. "CLD was an important part of my high school year because it made a huge impact on my life when it came to being professional and successful in the business world," she noted. "CLD influenced the way I conducted myself in college interviews, internships, and in the world after college."

Fleming was not the only one who was stimulated by the CLD experience. In a letter dated May 15, 1980, Tomkins wrote Hankinson to tell him how being a mentor affected her and that there really was something to the old adage, "If at first you don't succeed try, try again," when it came to finding a shadow experience for her charge.

"We gave it one more shot and we hit a bull's-eye," Tompkins said. "I wanted to thank you for your dedication to the objectives of the CLD and for permitting me to be part of your Advisory Council. There is one thing for sure—these students really make you work to keep ahead of them. . . . I wanted to share with you what becomes more obvious to me each day—if we expect students to learn that goals can be accomplished, then we must be willing to work along with them just as (if not more) determined as they are."

The Post-Secondary Path

In order to encourage their students to seek a post-secondary education, understand what college life was all about, and get them excited about their futures, the CLD implemented a number of programs and activities to set them on a path toward success.

In 1978 Schuyler Otteson, CLD board president, arranged a bus trip to Indiana University's Bloomington campus for program graduates so that they could tour the school and visit the famed Little 500 bicycle race. It was a popular and exciting event that became a regular part of the CLD's annual activities for a while, but it was hardly the only one that was centered on continuing education. The CLD also offered financial-aid seminars to help students and their families fill out the federal forms for financial assistance and understand what grants or scholarships might be available.

In 1980 the CLD also partnered with IUPUI's Continuing Studies department to offer a six-week Scholastic Aptitude Test prep program, which still exists. It is designed to help students improve their scores on the all-important College Board exam. Historically, minorities scored lower on the SAT than their Caucasian counterparts, but in the early 1980s those scores were lower than ever. By offering an SAT prep program, the CLD learned it could help boost a student's score by as many as forty points.

It was not enough, however, for the CLD to provide young people with appropriate role models, the opportunity for self-reflection, relevant life skills, the chance to shadow area professionals, and the desire to seek a college education. The organization also knew it was important to keep that minority talent close to home. The CLD created unique workshops in specific fields such as engineering, medicine, science, and law, and in 1987 went a step further to create the Business Orientation Project in cooperation with the IU School of Business.

The Business Orientation Project (still offered today) is an eleven-week course for graduates of the Self-Discovery/Career Exploration Project that focuses on business careers. In 1988 the CLD established the College Intern Project, an initiative for high school graduates that matched an incoming college freshman with a local business in order to help them get their foot in the door of their chosen field, gain experience, and allow firms to get acquainted with the type of talent the CLD was producing through its efforts.

"It's no secret that when the CLD began, its goal was to identify promising African American talent

Board member Jackie Greenwood and (far left) CLD alumni Victor Bush ('87)

Bill West facilitating early CLD class

At right, CLD alumni Doctor Jennifer Siegel ('81)

Doctor LaForrest Garner, Early Role Model Program

and encourage them to enroll in the IU School of Business. It was even in that first grant proposal that was sent to the Lilly Endowment," said Thomas A. King, CLD board chairman and retired president and CEO of the Indiana State Museum and Historic Sites. As a CLD board member since 1983 and a former president of the Eli Lilly and Company Foundation, King acknowledged that there was an unspoken partnership of sorts among the CLD, Lilly, and IU, as many of the organizers had ties to all three entities. However, as the program developed, CLD leaders realized more could be done. "They saw there was application in all kinds of fields besides business and thanks to the quality of kids they were producing, other colleges and universities began to take notice of their program," said King.

The CLD not only introduced its students to a world beyond high school, but it also gave them the chance to apply their leadership skills within the organization by arranging trips to King's Island, summer picnics, holiday parties, and creating the CLD Alumni Association. The association is a group of working professionals, college, and high school students who completed the CLD's Self-Discovery/Career Exploration Project and wanted to remain connected to the organization by volunteering their time, talent, and treasure to the organization's initiatives. They also contributed to the CLD's quarterly newsletter, *Briefs*, that was designed to keep alumni and other interested parties abreast of activities happening with the organization. Issues contained updates from the president, upcoming

events, alumni spotlights, and articles written by CLD students and members of the Young Adult Advisory Council.

A Few Good Men

Television icon Oprah Winfrey once said that when you "empower a black man, you empower families. You empower his wife. You empower sons. You empower daughters . . . you light up the world." This belief is shared by the CLD and its leaders, who knew from the very start how important it was to recruit and retain a few good men to its programs. Although there were a lot of young men participating in the Self-Discovery/Career Exploration Project at first, in subsequent years their enrollment dropped off, resulting in the number of participating females to far exceed the number of

Sergeant Kendale Adams and Major Phil Burton, CLD alumni and facilitator

males. In order to combat the issue, the CLD made a concentrated effort to reach out to this crucial demographic.

The result was Project MR (Male Responsibility), a four-week program for junior high and high school boys who were not quite ready for the lessons of the Self-Discovery/ Career Exploration program, but needed something that would focus on what it meant to be a man while discovering the values, skills, lifestyle choices, and work ethic, along with the consequences that come with poor decision-making. Initiated in 1991, its participants learned to make a difference in their own lives, families, and community, as well as the larger world, while coping with those challenging situations that seek to compromise their efforts.

"I loved the fact that CLD expanded their programming to include Project MR," said Doctor Jacqueline

Greenwood. "We had a similar program at Arlington called the A-Men, which was the brainchild of Howard Stevenson and designed for those young men who were on the cusp of dropping out. We had volunteers within the community who would come and teach them how to be young men and believe in themselves in hopes that they could turn their lives around."

Project MR was originally held on the Arlington campus on Saturday afternoons and was so successful that a similar program for young women was created a few years later. CLD president Dennis Bland (CLD '82) had served as a facilitator with the program and said it was important for the community to be very intentional about being aspirational where black men are concerned. "We have to acknowledge where our males are coming from," he noted, "before we can implement solutions. I think

one of the biggest challenges where our young men are concerned that we rarely talk about is this total sense of abandonment that so many males face. If you look at the demographics and you see numbers that say anywhere from 50 to 70 and 80 percent of African American males do not live with their fathers, that's a profound social and familial hurt, and a number of males tend to act out that hurt in different ways."

When they participate in Project MR, young men meet high-achieving males who have walked in their shoes, have knowledge to pass along, and can give that encouragement and guidance young men need at such a critical time of their life.

"In the beginning . . . there is some hesitancy, but as they begin to interact with the male role models . . . these young people begin to embrace those males not only because they have achieved . . . but because they have taken the time to say, 'I really do care about your life and your future' and that goes a long way helping these young people succeed," Bland said.

Broadening Horizons

By the latter part of the 1980s, the CLD understood it was not only the high school students of central Indiana who needed its support. The world was changing and there was a growing need in the community to find answers and solutions for a widening range of young people. The CLD had to start reaching students long before high school in order to help get them on the right path. The organization adapted its pilot program to reach middle school students and then again to include fourth and fifth graders. Today the CLD offers fifteen programs that reach out to a variety of grade levels, are geared for both genders, and encourage young people to develop leadership skills and a life plan no matter what their age. These programs include:

- **Parents Chat (1995)** A program for the parents of students in the fourth to twelfth grades to help themselves and their students to achieve a healthy lifestyle and to reach their educational goals. Group discussions allow parents to share knowledge about how to help their children develop into healthy, productive, and responsible adults.
- **Rawls Scholars Medicine Initiative (2002)** Provides students interested in a career in medicine the chance to get up close and interact with medical professionals and students in the community.
- **Success Prep (2003)** A high school readiness program intended to give incoming freshmen the chance to understand the importance of a good grade point average, develop solid study skills, and be able to self-advocate throughout the eight semesters of high school.
- **Imani Book Club (2004)** A six-week summer reading program for fourth through twelfth graders that strives to improve literacy and nurture an appreciation for the written word.
- **Precious Miss (2007)** Originally known as the Female Program, Precious Miss is an eight-week program for girls in the sixth to eighth grades that strives to empower them with valuable knowledge, a greater sense of self-esteem, self-worth, and achievement in order to set themselves up for success in life.

Early Self-Discovery graduation

Early Self-Discovery graduation, Arlington High School

- **Junior Self-Discovery/Career Exploration Project (2008)** A program designed for fourth through sixth graders to help them identify their interests, values, personality, and what they want to be when they grow up. Students interact with their peers and skilled facilitators to equip themselves with the tools they need for success in school, work, and life.

Victor Bush (CLD'87) said not only does the CLD have dynamic programming designed to help kids stay in school and go on to college, but it also provides role models in every program who help set a standard for kids and encourage them to remain involved in the community. Ever since he graduated from Lawrence North High School, Bush has been giving back, whether it is serving as a facilitator for CLD programs or through his work as a district behavior consultant at the Metropolitan School District of Lawrence Township. In 2015 he was the recipient of the CLD's Distinguished Alumni Award.

Bush said he learned so much through the original Self-Discovery/Career Exploration Project and he loves the way in which the CLD has expanded over the years to create programs that serve kids of all ages. "Everyone who comes into the building feels welcome and they come back each week because they have fun, engaging learning experiences that are not boring," he said. "It is a true passion of mine to work with young adults and to see the fruit of that labor five or ten years down the line when they are off doing great things. That's what the programming at the CLD does—it teaches you how to win at the game of life."

Facilitator and students

Facilitator Lee Christian

> "I believed in my heart he was right for the job."
>
> *Mildred Ball*

Chapter 6 Passing the Torch

When Dennis Bland received a letter inviting him to join the Center for Leadership Development in the fall of 1982, he ignored it. Although he was flattered to be identified as someone with leadership potential, the Broad Ripple High School senior was already the president of the student council and a member of the varsity basketball team. He did not have the time or the inclination to take on another extracurricular activity.

A few weeks later, a follow-up letter arrived in his mailbox. This time, instead of merely extending an invitation to join the youth development program, it chastised him for his lack of response. It was an admonition that caused Bland to bristle with indignation and reconsider his decision about the CLD

program. The teenager had no way of knowing that his change of heart would ultimately change his life forever.

A Transformative Experience

As the son of sharecroppers who picked cotton in the Deep South before relocating to Indianapolis, Bland was the first person in his family to earn the equivalent of a middle school education, let alone a high school diploma. Naturally, the concept of attending college and obtaining a degree seemed like a far-off, distant notion and one his parents could not help him achieve. However, his father firmly believed in the power of education and knew if his son were somehow afforded the opportunity to study at a university, he should take it and not

let any roadblocks stand in his way. He knew it would be the young man's key to getting ahead in life.

Bland was not as confident. "Our experiences have a lot to do with our own history," he said. "If you grow up in an environment where higher education and a professional career are part of your lexicon, then it's more likely a tangible goal. If you don't, it's more like a leap of faith."

To his credit, Bland took that leap of faith by enrolling in the CLD's youth development program and taking part in the Self-Discovery/Career Exploration Project course. Like others teens who participated in the thirteen-week sessions, he made a connection between who he was, where he wanted to be in life, and how he intended to get there. He said

The CLD Principles for Success

Infused in every CLD program are the organization's Principles for Success, a five-point holistic approach designed to help students maximize their talents and learn valuable lessons while reaching for the stars. The CLD's five Principles for Success are:

1 Character Development Respect for self and others, integrity, discipline, purpose, and other traits vital to success.

2 Educational Excellence Encouraging youth to pursue the highest level of education that they can.

3 Leadership Effectiveness Training, practical experiences to positively lead and serve peers in school, churches, organizations, businesses, neighborhoods, and community.

4 Community Service Serving the people you lead. Learning the purpose and process of being a servant leader to those in need.

5 Career Achievement Helping youth by exposing them to the many careers available to them, educating students about the education, knowledge, and skills that may be required to realize their dreams.

the CLD gave him a holistic understanding of college, not just as an avenue for education, but also as preparation for adulthood. The classes taught him how to interact with others on a professional level, advocate for himself, and gave him new role models to emulate, such as former CLD assistant director and class facilitator Holbrook Hankinson. "Holbrook Hankinson really was the 'gold standard' and everything I wanted to be when I grew up," Bland said. "By taking advantage of the CLD opportunity, I was able to work with him and others who had 'been there, done that' and had some wisdom to share. The CLD program was transformative for me. It helped me see things in a whole new way."

Giving Back

After receiving his high school diploma in the spring of 1983, Bland attended his mentor's alma mater, DePauw University in Greencastle, graduating with a degree in economics in 1987. He returned to Indianapolis to begin his professional career and accepted a position as an underwriter with

Former Indianapolis mayor Bart Peterson with Stephen Stitle, Henry Bundles, and Dennis Bland

the American States Insurance Company. He also returned to the CLD to serve as a volunteer facilitator, mentoring to a new group of students who were in the same position he was only a few short years before.

"I was fresh out of DePauw and I wanted to give back. I wanted to share and spread what I had learned with the youth of the community. I wanted them to foster a deep and abiding consciousness of the power of education. I could never have imagined that my earnest desire to help others would become my life's work," he said.

But that is exactly what happened. For twenty-six weeks a year Bland worked with minority youth in CLD cohorts, and in 1989 he was invited to join the organization's board of directors. He remained active in many of the CLD's initiatives even as he returned to school to pursue his law degree at Indiana University's Indianapolis campus, opened his own practice, and eventually became a staff attorney with the Indiana Department of Insurance.

In 1994 Bland felt called to do even more. After serving as a facilitator for nearly a decade, he noticed several shifts in the minority youth culture and was taken aback by its impact on students. There were an ever-growing number of problems and gaps that were preventing these kids from being ready for success at the high school level, and it appeared that no one was doing anything to change it. "In order to assuage my conscious, I took what I had gleaned from being a facilitator and began writing a book about what I saw and what could be done to change it," he said.

President Dennis Bland (top row, center) as facilitator

That manuscript became the curriculum for the CLD's Success Prep program. Influenced in part by statistics that identified black youths as having the lowest academic performance of any demographic, as well as the highest dropout rate, Success Prep is a high school readiness and enrichment program designed to help incoming freshmen get a strong start. Participants in Success Prep learn how to study, how much to study, how to improve their grade point average, and how to ask for help if they need it. The program also digs deep to counter the adverse messaging students receive on a daily basis from their peers, teachers, family, and society.

Bland said it's not always easy to compete for the heart and mind of a teenager, but if a Success Prep facilitator can gain access, they can influence those hearts and minds in a positive way. "If all children

get is negativity, then there really is no reason to thrive, grow, and excel. They won't pursue their potential or set meaningful, realistic goals," he said. "Success Prep is one of the proactive steps undertaken by the CLD to improve the academic and social performance of our youths."

Mr. President

In late 1998 CLD founding president Henry Bundles informed the board that he was stepping down from his position after twenty-three years and a lifetime of community service. He had been involved with the CLD since its inception and under his leadership the organization had impacted the lives of thousands, but at the age of seventy-three he was ready to pass the torch to a new generation in order to enjoy his golden years alongside his

President Dennis Bland and CLD alumni Jennine Hunter

Bland speaking at graduation

second wife, Helen Baker. (Bundles had previously been a widower.) "I think it's time to get out and let young people with more energy than I continue the work," he said.

It would be a tall order to find anyone to fill Bundles's shoes and legacy, and Bland was honored to join the committee in search of the CLD's next president. He had no designs on the position for himself. He was happily practicing law, facilitating classes, and serving on the board, but during a meeting to discuss potential candidates he was surprised when fellow board member Mildred Ball wondered aloud why they were looking at outside candidates when the most qualified person for the position was sitting at that very table. "I kind of joked and said, 'You know Mildred, I think you're right. You should apply,'" he recalled, knowing full well who she had in mind.

Naturally Bland was humbled that anyone would think him to be a worthy successor to Bundles, but he did not put his name forward. Over the next few months, Ball repeated her assertion that he would make a great CLD president, and one day she stopped Bland after a meeting at the Indianapolis Power and Light Company on Monument Circle to make a final appeal. She told him no one knew the organization the same way he did. He was a product of the program. He was a volunteer. He served as a member of the board and was a highly respected member of the community. "You are the right person for this position, but if you are dead set against it, I will never mention it again," she told him.

Ball said her belief stemmed from watching Bland remain connected to the CLD even after he completed the program and went on to achieve so

much in his professional career. "Dennis was the total package," she recalled. "He didn't have a big ego and he was not full of himself, but he was a wonderful example of what the program could do for someone. He was dedicated to the CLD and I knew he was perfect for it."

Unwilling to cast aside such a conviction, the deeply religious Bland promised Ball that he would pray about the issue. He did pray and he weighed the pros and cons, but as the day of the application deadline approached, he did not feel he had received a clear-cut answer. Torn, he called one of his sisters to discuss the quandary and she told him to go for it, if he applied and they said no, then he had God's answer on the issue. If he did not put his name in, he would never know if it was God's plan for his life or not. He saw the logic and turned in his application and credentials.

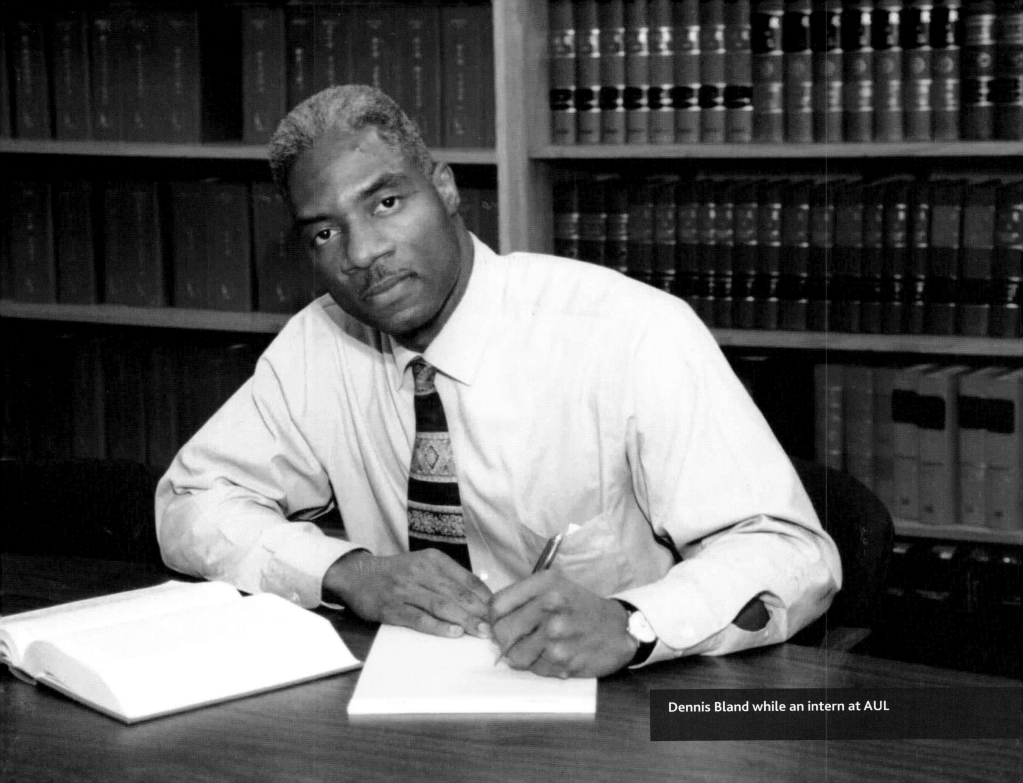

Dennis Bland while an intern at AUL

Bland with project facilitators

However, despite Bland's strong qualifications, the board decided to offer the position to another candidate. Bland was sad, of course, but he accepted the decision and continued his work in the legal field, as well as his service with the CLD. A few weeks later, he received a voice mail from board chairman Stephen Stitle, president of National City Bank (now PNC), who told him that the other candidate turned down the position and that it was his if he still wanted it. Bland could not believe the turn of events. "I must have played that message ten times," he said.

When it was announced that Bland would be the CLD's second president, Bundles said he was pleased with the board's decision and wished Bland nothing but the best in his new role. "Over time, I think Dennis will do a fine job," he said. It was high praise coming from a man whose efforts were still

speaking to and through two generations of young people and who would be named a Living Legend by the Indiana Historical Society in 2005.

Since taking the CLD's helm, Bland has helped to expand its youth-development programs and works tirelessly to spread awareness about what he feels is often the best-kept secret in Indianapolis. He was appointed to the Indiana Commission for Higher Education in 2004 and elected chairman of the commission in 2014. He has helped enhance the CLD's reputation as a one of the strongest, most viable vehicles the community has for propelling minority youth into the world of personal development and career success. In 2016 he was awarded the Sagamore of the Wabash, one of the state's highest honors, by Governor Mike Pence (now Vice President Pence.)

John Myrland, former president of the Indianapolis Chamber of Commerce, CLD board member, and pastor of the McCordsville United Methodist Church, was a personal friend of Bland's who said that the extraordinary thing about him is that he does not have to be doing this at all. "He could be making a lot of money working for a big law firm, perhaps giving some time to the CLD as a volunteer and telling his friends about how he helped some high school kids today," noted Myrland, "but that's not Dennis. He knows God has blessed him with wonderful gifts, and he has chosen to go where God led him."

Myrland said Bland's story may not be unique, but what makes his story truly meaningful is that he is planting in others the same values and characteristics he possesses so that when he is ready to move on, there will be someone else to take his place and perhaps one of the students he previously mentored. "What a marvelous example of a servant leader," he said.

Chapter 7 A New Home

Roman philosopher Gaius Plinus Secundus once said, "Home is where the heart is," and for the past four decades the Center for Leadership Development has held its programs and events in a number of locations. It also changed its base of operations several times. However, no matter if "home" was a low-rent, multipurpose space or a gleaming state-of-the-art facility, the "heart" of the organization remains the same: to afford central Indiana youth and their parents a broad spectrum of program experiences unrivaled in range, depth, and scope.

Humble Beginnings

When the organization's board of directors met on October 26, 1977, it did not have a name for its infant initiative nor a formal curriculum, let alone a place to call its own. As the board gathered in Parlor E of the Indianapolis Athletic Club, it created and approved the CLD name, outlined its primary objectives, and drafted a job description for its president. Finding a formal office was not on the agenda.

Four months later the group reconvened. Henry Bundles was installed as the CLD's founding president, and he announced that he had located a 385-square-foot space in the Union Federal Building in downtown Indianapolis to serve as the organization's first administrative offices for a monthly rent of $232.60. It was small and needed work, but it would suffice for the time being. The next order of business was to find a place in which they could launch the CLD's youth development program and hold its first classes.

Thankfully, Eli Lilly and Company had the answer. In addition to the Lilly Endowment offering the funding, the company offered the organization the use of a company-owned A-frame building on the south side of downtown Indianapolis that was also used by the Boy Scouts of America. "We used that Boy Scout building for the first few semesters of our program, but it was very cold in the winter months," Holbrook Hankinson recalled. "Not only that, but some of the students felt it was a little out of the way. It wasn't long before we started searching for another location."

CLD office locations past and present

1. 45 North Pennsylvania Street, #315
2. 1036 North Capitol
3. 1812 North Meridian Street
4. 3536 Washington Boulevard
5. 2425 Doctor Martin Luther King Jr. Street

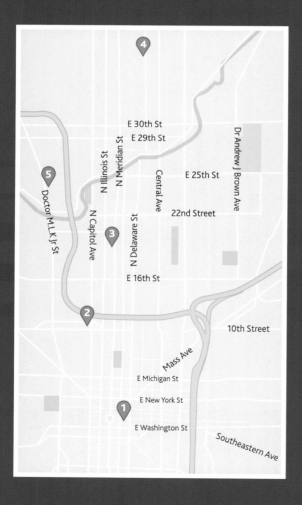

Intersection of current CLD location

That search led to a seemingly endless array of low-to-no-rent facilities whose owners and organizations believed in what the CLD was doing and were willing to supply the organization with adequate space. One of those facilities was the Claver Community Center located at 3110 Sutherland Avenue. The Claver Center was a 23,500 square-foot building that was home to the Knights and Ladies of Saint Peter Claver, the largest historically African American Catholic lay organization in the United States. The Claver Center had a ballroom, lounge, and dining room, along with several small meeting spaces. Best of all, the center only charged the CLD $1 per year to hold its classes on site.

Hankinson said that naturally there was a catch to getting such a great deal on the rent. "If they had a paying customer, we would get pushed to another room, and sometimes they would be so full that we had to hold classes in the kitchen," he laughed. "Still, it was this great organization that was willing to support us with some much needed space."

The CLD did not mind its arrangement with the Claver Center, and it certainly used the facility for more than just the youth development program, using it for training sessions, Young Adult Advisory Meetings, Christmas parties, and other events. In time, however, that connection ended. After having to expand its offices in the Union Federal Building

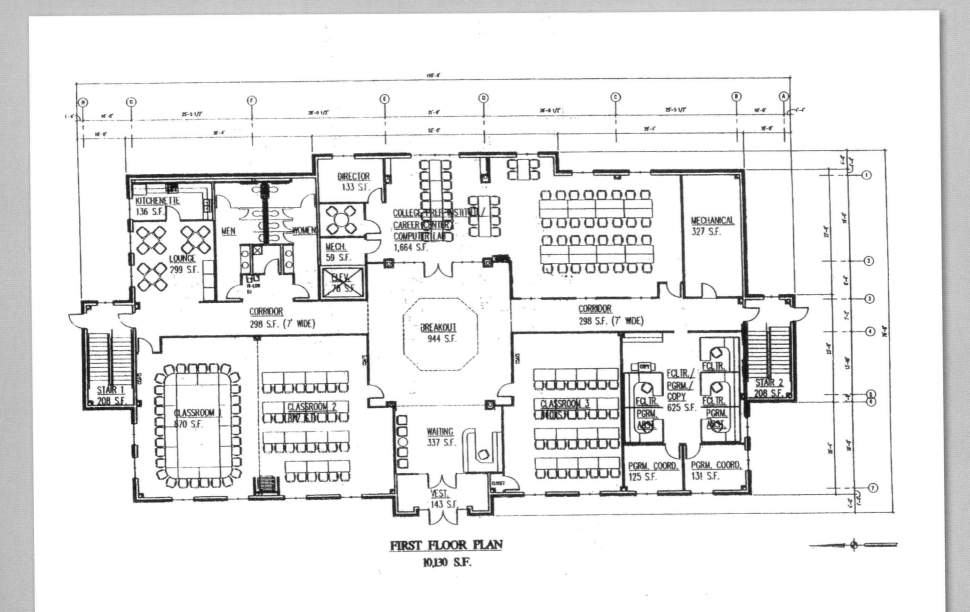

FIRST FLOOR PLAN
10,130 S.F.

Blackburn Associates Architects schematic of CLD building floor plan

Artist's rendering of CLD building

to accommodate its storage needs, the CLD decided its next location should be large enough to combine offices with storage and classroom space. In 1982 it found the perfect spot: the Stutz Building at 1036 North Capitol.

Hankinson, who started out as a volunteer facilitator with the program before being hired as the CLD's assistant director, said he remembered the Stutz Building with great fondness. It was the kind of place where everyone pitched in to do the necessary work to keep the place looking nice and the

office running efficiently. "I remember Barbara Garrett, Alicia Anderson, and myself waxing the floors each week because they were kind of old and they looked bad," he said. "I didn't think anything of doing it because my dad used to have a job cleaning a bowling alley and he used to take me with him so I was used to that kind of thing."

But five years later the CLD had outgrown the Stutz space. By the spring of 1987 the organization's youth development program had met every benchmark it had set for itself, had exceeded all

expectations, and was expanding its programming. Out of the 1,085 students that had taken part in its Self-Discovery/Career Exploration Project by the CLD's tenth anniversary and finished high school, 873 had enrolled in college, giving the organization an 80 percent success rate. Another 118 were enrolled in the program at the time so it was obvious to everyone that the organization was only getting bigger and better. As time went on, the board agreed that a move was in order and that summer the CLD relocated to a 4,000-square-foot area at

NEWSMAKERS

$1.4 MILLION GRANT: Eli Lilly and Company Chief Financial Officer Derica Rice (l) and Lilly President and COO John Lechleiter display a check for $1.4 million for the Center for Leadership Development (CLD) in downtown Indianapolis. The gift from the Eli Lilly company will help build the new Lilly Center for Leadership Development that will expand the organization's capacity and further enrich its youth programming. The CLD is a non-profit organization aimed at helping minority youth in Central Indiana to become future professionals and business and community leaders.

Eli Lilly check presentation

1812 North Meridian Street, five minutes from the heart of downtown.

Busting at the Seams

Although there were times when the offices and classrooms needed repairs and improvements, upgrades, and renovations, the Meridian office provided the CLD with enough room to grow and thrive for nearly a decade. However, in 1995 space was once again at a premium, and another move

was in the offing. Rather than look for a rental, board members began searching for available properties that might meet the Center's needs and budget. They ultimately found a spot that just might fit the bill: a ten-year-old edifice at 3536 Washington Boulevard. "Henry [Bundles], Bill Mays, and I found the building, and after we talked about it and had the engineering guys look into it we thought it would be a good move for the CLD, but we didn't have any money," said Bill West.

The agent for the property was Gus Miller, and the CLD worked with him to assume the mortgage from Merchants Bank, using a capital gift from a private donor to cover the seller's equity. Unfortunately, it was not enough, and Mays approached the loan officer to find out what needed to be done. He offered to secure the mortgage by putting up a $50,000 certificate of deposit. The loan officers agreed to the terms, and the CLD organized a fund drive to pay off the rest of the debt. With two tenants already installed in the building, the monthly income would help keep the CLD's budget manageable and help offset the additional costs.

However, there was a looming question: how could the CLD make the best use of the space so that it would not outgrow the building in a year or two? Ruth Iliff had the answer. She donated the space planning division of the Boehringer Mannheim Corporation (today Roche Diagnostics) to evaluate the place and suggest ways to maximize efficiency and note any interior/exterior improvements it might need. With the CLD's twentieth anniversary approaching, the board launched a capital

campaign to address any renovations the building needed. Over the past two decades more than 4,200 students had taken part in the CLD's flagship program, as well as its other initiatives at the time. The community was very aware of how vital the organization was, and they were very generous with their support. But ten years later the organization needed to relocate again. Everyone hoped this move might be the CLD's last.

The Lilly CLD Achievement Center

By 2007 the CLD expanded its offerings to include most of the programs it has today. The board hired Dennis Bland as the organization's president

when Bundles retired in 2000, and in its thirty-year history the Center had touched more than fifteen thousand lives. Most of the CLD graduates who finished high school went on to pursue post-secondary, graduate, and/or doctoral degrees, and many came back to serve as role models for the next generation. There was no question that the CLD had established a solid track record of empowering young people to excel in academics, college, career, and life. It was a beacon of hope for young people throughout central Indiana, but the more kids who flocked to its torch, the more difficult it became to accommodate everyone. "We are filled to capacity . . . beyond capacity actually," said Tamiko Jordan,

Photos of CLD building construction

Derica Rice, Eli Lilly and Company and CLD board member

Bob Bowen, former CLD board chair

who was vice president in charge of programming for the CLD at the time.

With a $250,000 grant from the Lilly Endowment, the board launched another capital campaign in hopes of raising enough money to begin construction on a new facility that would combine the best features of a challenging educational environment with a nurturing, culturally sensitive setting. The board raised $3.6 million, but was still short of its $5 million goal. Then, unexpectedly, the CLD received a gift it never could have imagined.

According to Bland, Marvin White was a Lilly employee and the father of a child involved in CLD programming. He traveled a lot for work and had not been able to attend any of the parent-orientation sessions. But when he did, he became intrigued by what the CLD was doing, and he wanted to help. Unbeknownst to the organization, White had some influence within the Lilly corporation and, together with his colleague Derica Rice, was able to leverage the resources that resulted in a $1.2 million grant for the new state-of-the-art building at a dream location: 2425 Doctor Martin Luther King Jr. Street.

"Lilly has been a supporter since the beginning and has remained a true partner throughout the years," Bland said in a press release. "Together, we are demonstrating our mutual commitment to delivering bold answers for our youth and community."

John Lechleiter, Lilly president and CEO, said the CLD's emphasis on building character, improving education, giving back to the community, and encouraging leadership and integrity is consistent with the values Lilly supports and desires of its employees. "We are fortunate to have many CLD alumni working with us at Lilly demonstrating these important attributes," said Lechleiter. "We support a variety of educational programs in Indiana and nationally to ensure we can continually deliver on our mission to provide medicines that help people live longer, healthier lives—future innovation is in the hands of our brightest youth."

Designed by Blackburn Associates and built by Davis and Associates, the Lilly CLD Achievement Center is a 20,000-square-foot building that includes several flexible classrooms and comfortable study spaces that can accommodate 150 people at a time. There is also the College Prep Institute, a college resource center and career center with thirty computer terminals compared to the one classroom and eight terminals that were in the previous building, as well as room for the College Prep Institute. The new space also features administrative offices, a central atrium, and land for future expansion.

Bland said he believed that the new building, for which ground was broken on October 3, 2007, and programs would "elevate Indianapolis students by teaching them to think about their education like they've never thought about it before. With the improvements, they have more resources to take their education seriously and go on to be contributors to society."

In April 2009 the CLD held a ribbon-cutting ceremony at the new building, which featured an invocation by Bishop T. Garrett Benjamin of Light of the World Christian Church, comments from CLD chairman Robert L. Bowen, founding board

Amos Brown and State Senator Glen Howard

member Joseph A. Slash, Capital Campaign Co-Chair Thomas King, remarks from former Mayor of Indianapolis Bart Peterson and CLD President Bland, as well as a dedication prayer offered by Suffragan Bishop Charles M. Finnell of Christ Temple Apostolic Faith Assembly. Rice and White were on hand representing the Eli Lilly and Company. Afterwards, guests were invited to tour the new facility, enjoy refreshments, and learn more about the programs the CLD offered the youth of Indianapolis.

Barbara Neal (CLD '80) said she was thrilled that students would be able to take advantage of the CLD opportunity in such an up-to-the-minute building designed to grow and evolve with them. "It's almost as if the torch had been lit again for a whole new generation of young people who face as many challenges as we did," she said.

> "We are very intentional about educating the whole person."
>
> *Dennis Bland*

Chapter 8 The College Prep Institute

Although the Center for Leadership Development means a great many things to a great many people, at its core the CLD is an educational institution focused on values and character building and every one of its programs has academic and post-secondary readiness components. The Imani Book Club, for example, promotes literacy success for students in grades four to twelve, while the Precious Miss and Project MR programs are initiatives in which students discover the academic and life skills that will lead to scholastic and career success. The Business Orientation Project allows students to see how corporate America works through experiential learning, and the Self-Discovery/Career Exploration Project acts as a live-action Global Positioning System, giving

a young person's life direction while helping them navigate the journey. However, no other CLD initiative is more focused on post-secondary education readiness and career success and fulfillment than the College Prep Institute.

Located within the Lilly CLD Achievement Center, the CPI was established to be a large-scale, holistic, post-secondary readiness and completion resource center helping students be admitted to college, persist, and graduate. It was created to support the community's need to address the pervasive educational crisis of far too many African American youth failing academically, dropping out of school, and having significantly low college graduation rates. Since its inception, the CPI's focus has been

to increase significantly the number of youth fully equipped to achieve three foundational college goals: admission, persistence, and graduation. The CPI prepares its participants for the rigors, expectations, and requirements of the post-secondary world so that they can successfully earn their degree or certificate from a college, university, or training academy.

At the CPI's ribbon-cutting ceremony in 2011, CLD president Dennis Bland said he is one of those people who believe that a college education can be transformative in the purist form of the word. It is not only life and career changing for the individual, but it also can profoundly influence one's peers, family, and community. "There are several reports and studies documenting the many benefits of earning a college degree or credential," he said. "It is not common knowledge that those who earn a four-year degree earn at least $1 million more over their work life than someone who has not . . . but in fact, the benefits of the well-educated far exceed dollars, and our community needs a fully-equipped, comprehensive resource center that is solely dedicated to the exhaustive promotion and advancement of academic and college preparation for youth, parents, and families."

A Community Resource Center

The CPI's roots go back to the earliest days of the CLD when the organization began holding special Saturday morning Scholastic Aptitude Test prep sessions for students, as well as workshops for families in order to help them understand the college admission process and how to fill out those all important financial aid forms. As the CLD evolved, there was a need to offer more of a community-based resource center that would strategically propel high school and college graduation rates in the nation while building a culture of scholarship and learning for the youth of central Indiana and

CLD board member Bob Bowen and CLD students

beyond, all free of charge. Bland said he would love nothing more than for the CLD to help the Indianapolis African American community enjoy the highest high school graduation rates in the nation.

"We want all of our young people and parents to understand that, irrespective of the goal, there has to be a commitment to excellence and preparation for something beyond the secondary level," Bland said. "No matter if that is a two-year, four-year, or certificate program, our focus is to make sure they are comprehensively ready for whatever the next step might be."

The CPI is a one-stop, self-contained college resource center that is open to the community and staffed with licensed guidance counselors who meet with individuals in order to evaluate their academic standing and determine how they can move forward. They assess a student in core subject areas, identify their strengths and weaknesses, examine the social and personal issues that may be affecting their education, discover which career paths interest them, and help them develop a plan to meet those goals. When a CLD student or community member comes to the CPI with their head hanging low over a poor grade point average, the counselors are ready to put them at ease and reassure them that all hope is not lost.

"CPI counselors work with students from where they are, but there is some loving judgment that comes along with that," said Bland. "Our counselors give individuals an honest evaluation of where they are and what they need to do to change course. They look at where a child is struggling, help them think about the possibilities, and then assist them in creating a plan to get that individual where they want to be. "

Making the Transition

The transition from high school to college is not an easy one, but it's even harder for minority students who are often ill prepared for the challenges ahead. According to statistics from the Indiana Department of Education, approximately 24 percent of African American students who enroll in college will go on to earn a bachelor's degree. This is why the CLD believes it is essential that students have a solid strategy for academic success and that they understand what resources are available should

the need arise. The CPI is not a one-time shop for college guidance that students come to once during their high school career, but it is a one-stop resource they should plan to visit over and over again.

Doctor Robert L. Bowen, founder and chairman of Bowen Engineering Corporation, was the CLD board chair when the CPI was established, and he knew

College Prep Institute launch

CPI Services include:

- Free one-on-one licensed guidance counseling to assess school risk factors, career interests, and to create a post-secondary education plan for the student.

- Reading, language arts, and math grade-level assessments to determine a student's current level of learning.

- Free tutoring services and access to reading specialists.

- Weekend and evening hours in order to be accessible to students and parents.

- Workshops and Parents Chat designed around parent and student success, college obstacles, and community concerns.

- Information on other CLD programs that support college preparation and career goal achievement.

- Career assessments and college searches.

- Assistance in finding internships and scholarships.

Board chair Tom King

Institute launch materials

how hard it was for young people to thrive at the post-secondary level. Even if they made the grades necessary to be accepted at a college or university, they had trouble getting acclimated to their new environment. "I knew kids who said they were miserable the entire time they were at college, so it is important to get them ready for that next step. The CPI and the CLD are very committed to that idea, and they are doing so many good things so that every kid can come out a winner," he said.

It's not merely enough to be accepted at a college or university, but one has to know how to thrive in some of the "unspoken" areas of the post-high

school world. Parents may or may not be able to help in this endeavor, and it is important that students know what they can expect not only in the classroom but in social situations as well. The CPI and other workshops offer a holistic look at the college life that goes beyond classes, financial aid, and peer pressure.

Amy Conrad-Warner, vice chancellor for community engagement at Indiana University–Purdue University at Indianapolis, said that as a longtime partner of the CLD the university knows that when students are prepared and excited to go to college, they will make that transition and will perform very

well. "This kind of institute makes a huge difference to their success, and we want them to be successful and to graduate with us from IUPUI," she said.

Although everyone has teaching and learning at their high schools, unfortunately not everyone has people who care about them and are willing to take the time to explain what it means to go to college and be truly prepared in plain and simple terms. That is where the CPI can help. Because of its accessibility, counselors at the CPI can go over and above what occurs in a traditional high school guidance department in order to help students shore up less than stellar grades, stay on track, and choose the courses that may lead to the college or university of their choice.

They also emphasize the time management/study skills taught in other CLD programs and help students navigate difficult relationships, personal issues, and learn to be self-advocates. Just as there are services and accommodations available for elementary, middle, and high school students

Each spring, CLD alums receive scholarships through the organization's college and university partners. These awards are given out during the Minority Achievers Awards and Scholarship Gala and typically top approximately $3 million annually. These partners include:

- Ball State University
- Butler University
- Cornerstone University
- DePauw University
- Earlham College
- Franklin College
- Hanover College
- Indiana State University
- Indiana University
- Indiana University–Purdue University at Indianapolis
- Ivy Tech Community College of Indiana
- Manchester University
- Marian University
- North Carolina A&T State University
- Purdue University
- University of Indianapolis
- Vincennes University
- Wabash College
- Cathedral High School
- Brebeuf Jesuit Preparatory High School
- University High School
- University of Notre Dame
- Saint Mary-of-the-Woods College
- University of Evansville
- Saint Richard Episcopal School

with varying needs and challenges, these same services are also available at the college level as well. However, unlike high school in which parents, grandparents, and other caregivers are the ones to request such options, the onus is on the student at the post-secondary level, and they must know how to speak up for themselves. "It's all about preparing them for the road ahead," said CPI director Lena Hill (CLD '99). "We want them to be the best they can be."

Students at computers in the College Prep Institute

Opportunities abound

The CLD and CPI offer a number of workshops and seminars throughout the year designed to help students and their families understand what it takes to be admitted into college, persist, and graduate. They tell them about available scholarship opportunities and how to navigate the potential pitfalls along the way. These special events often include noted guest speakers, college/university representatives, and additional resources in order to give students the knowledge they need to take that next step.

Imagine 1,500 students (grades eight to twelve) from cities and schools throughout Indiana and their parents congregating in one place to gain a comprehensive understanding of the entire college readiness process. That's what the CLD's Annual College Prep Conference and College Fair is all about. The College Prep Conference and College Fair helps families learn how they can help their child succeed in high school, apply for college admission, fill out the Free Application for Federal Student Aid, enroll, thrive, and, most importantly, graduate from college with a degree and gain employment in the career of their choice.

In the CLD Emerging Scholars one-day program, high school students and their families learn about the millions of dollars available in scholarship opportunities, their eligibility requirements, and how to apply for them. Participants also have the chance to learn how to write, revise, and proofread their college application résumé and essays while meeting with representatives from a number of schools in a college fair setting. This event is particularly beneficial for high school juniors and seniors who are getting ready for the post-secondary environment.

College Prep is an eight-week program designed for high school juniors, seniors, and incoming college freshmen to find out what it takes to be truly successful at the college level. Parents have a corresponding course they attend in order to learn how to empower and support their student. Through a hands-on approach, attendees are offered a comprehensive understanding of college admission and graduation requirements, how to choose the right school for the student, how to take the right courses for your particular major, how to develop solid study skills, and what to expect from the college experience. A lead facilitator oversees the class while a current college student serves as a mentor.

A Blessed Organization

In 2014 WTLC's Amos Brown broadcast his daily radio talk show from the CLD, taking calls from parents and alums of the organization, as well as highlighting the College Prep Institute and the services it provides. During the broadcast, a parent of a 2000 alum called in to say that his daughter had been a very troubled young lady as a teenager, but when his wife got her involved with the CLD it helped refocus her mind and get her going in the right direction. The caller said: "At first I thought, 'Here's another program, but I promise . . . it was a serious turning point for my daughter . . . it was their . . . concern and caring that really helped . . . now she is over at Ivy Tech and IUPUI doing great work and that was a major turnaround for her. . . . It is just a blessed organization."

Educator Doctor Steve Perry and students at 2016 College Prep Conference

The CPI also continues to offer its six-week SAT Prep course designed to help students study and master the "new" SAT, one of the primary factors colleges use to determine a student's eligibility. Former Hamilton Southeastern student Jeffery French (CLD '12) took part in some of CLD's college preparatory programming and said it made all the difference as he became a student at Purdue University. "I believe that I have always tried to strive for educational excellence, but CLD has instilled in me valuable study skills that I didn't possess [before]. These new study habits allowed me to do very well on my SAT on which I scored . . . a 2,220 [out of a score of 2,400]," he said.

A Family Affair

Of course, even if a student performs well on the SAT, applies to, and is accepted by a college or university, there is no guarantee that he or she will make it to graduation day. The post-secondary world is peppered with potential pitfalls, and it is

College Prep Institute ribbon cutting

Dennis Bland at College Prep Institute opening

important for families to know how to navigate those issues when and if they come up. The CPI's workshops are interactive events that cover the hidden costs of college, what college is really like (led by student facilitators), and how to support your student when they become overwhelmed.

The CLD and CPI believe that parental and familial support is critical to a student's overall success,

and that is why their presence is integrated into the CLD's youth development program. They are invited to a variety of workshops and programs designed to give them the resources they need to understand the college admission process and demystify some of the terms and concepts that may be new to them. In some cases, parents or guardians are required to participate.

If parents are unavailable to attend the special sessions, other family members are encouraged to step in. One CLD parent said when his schedule could not accommodate the meetings, the organization allowed grandparents, cousins, and extended relations to take his place. "They allow the whole family to be part of the program," he said.

> "It opened my eyes and expanded my horizons."
>
> *Steven Jones*

Chapter 9 The Impact of the Center for Leadership Development

If one were to dig below the surface of any successful organization, he or she would most likely find some kind of system designed to measure how effective its programs and initiatives are. The Center for Leadership Development is no different, and each year its staff compiles a comprehensive progress report that showcases success, charts growth, evaluates feedback, and identifies the organization's future needs. It is this report that enables the staff, administration, board, and volunteers to keep the CLD's mission going and plan for the years ahead.

However, that is only part of the story. Although the CLD enjoys a 95 percent high school graduation rate for its students and a 50 percent graduation rate for those who go on to attend college (based on reported data), the impact of the CLD goes far beyond the statistics and data that can be typed on an annual report or entered into a spreadsheet. While the organization continues to improve its methods of evaluation and strengthen its program structure to measure more effectively the outcomes of its offerings, the proof is in the lives that have been touched by CLD programming. It is in the personal stories of students who have been transformed by various offerings, the parents who watch their child flourish, the educators who see positive changes in academic progress, the mentors who see the difference they make in the lives of young people, and a community, including colleges, universities, and corporations, that are enriched by the emerging talent pool. That is the impact Henry Bundles and the other organizers hoped to achieve in 1977 and that is the impact that the Center continues to make to this day. "The CLD has a great message, and it makes a huge difference," said former board chair and current board member Bob Bowen.

Set Up for Success

When a child walks through the doors of the Lilly CLD Achievement Center, they know that they are entering a student-centered environment. They meet professional men and women who love them, care about their future, and want the best for them.

Project MR participants and CLD alumni and facilitator Ban Anderson in tug-of-war activity

These individuals have walked a mile or two in their shoes, have some knowledge to share, and because they have experienced success in their personal lives, they believe the student can achieve success as well.

"There is a strong expectation for success at CLD," said Dennis Bland. "It is not a place where someone comes and is merely told to straighten up and fly right, it is a standard and an expectation. The bar is much higher here. It's the reason everyone is taking

the time to work with them. Success is not a 'hope,' it is an expectation."

Steven Jones believes the CLD is an outstanding program that does not always get the credit it deserves. When he enrolled in the Self-Discovery/Career Exploration Project in 1981, he already possessed a strong work ethic that was supported by the concepts he learned at the Center. "It served as a foundation for where I stand today," he said.

After graduating from Arsenal Tech in 1983, Jones attended Wabash College and earned his degree in economics in 1987. He launched his professional career as a district sales manager for the *Indianapolis Star* and *Indianapolis News* before moving to the Indiana Department of Transportation and serving as the affirmative action director under former governor Evan Bayh. Eventually Jones made the transition to health care, becoming the human resources director for The HealthCare Group, LLC, and an employee relations executive at Methodist Hospital. Today he serves as the dean for professional development and the director of the Malcolm X Institute for Black Studies at Wabash College. "More than anything else, it opened my eyes and expanded my horizons," he said. "When I was in high school, I thought I wanted to be an engineer, but through the CLD I began to explore my options and found out that engineering might not be the right fit for me. I was much more of a people person."

Jones said that CLD mentors such as Henry Bundles, Helen Baker, and Holbrook Hankinson showed him what a minority male could be, and the program gave him the confidence he needed to go after his dreams. He said outside of the black church, the CLD is the greatest organization in the Indianapolis community, and he is proud to continue to serve it. "What transpired in the CLD created a sense of hope to individuals who were in that critical thirteen to fifteen age bracket, and now they serve students from the fourth grade on. I have made a point of giving back to the organization because they gave so much to me," he said.

Doctor Eugene White

Nikki Blaine

Very Valuable Tools

Not only do former students laud CLD programming and return to donate their time, talent, and treasure to the organization, but parents and educators also support the mission of the CLD. For some parents the Center is a program that turns their child's life around. For others, it underscores the values they are trying to impart, and for some parents the CLD becomes a family tradition.

Kelvin Wade (CLD '86) first learned about the CLD through his older cousins, who graduated from

the Self-Discovery/Career Exploration Project. His mother signed him up for the CLD's flagship course, and as he participated in the sessions he saw value in the curriculum and began to apply the lessons in his own life. "Mr. Bundles really honed in on a few things that stuck with me," he said. "At CLD we have a saying, 'In time, on time, every time, except when a little ahead of time and that's better time.' That really resonated with me. Although I have not always been able to do it, I always felt the pressure to be on time for things and finish what I start because of what I had been exposed to in the CLD."

After high school, Wade spent ten years in the military, serving in Desert Shield/Storm in the early 1990s; Fort Riley, Kansas; and Fort Sam Houston, Texas. When he returned to Indianapolis after his enlistment, he barely recognized the CLD. The organization had a new building, a new president, and was serving a larger population of students. But the lessons remained the same and as Wade got to know Bland and saw how the organization had grown, he wanted to get involved. Not only did he volunteer to participate in career fair events, but he also showed his financial support, served as president of the CLD Alumni Association, and made sure two sons also benefited from the program.

"Although I am well past my adolescent years and long into my adult life, I still think that program had the most influence on me," Wade said. "Through the CLD, kids get the benefit of being around professionals who look just like them and who show them that they can be more than athletes and rappers. Not that there is anything wrong with that, but there are other options. Through the CLD they learn that they can exercise their minds and be just as successful."

As a teenager, Nikki Blaine longed to be an attorney or a fashion designer. She learned to sew in a home economics class at Lawrence Central High School, but it was at the CLD that she learned to have a goal-oriented mindset and to be responsible at all times for making her dreams come true. After graduation, Blaine received a scholarship to the Indiana Institute of Technology, where she earned several business degrees. She continued designing on the side and thanks to her hard work and persistence today she is the owner of Nikki Blaine Couture in Zionsville, has won multiple awards for her work, and has dressed such luminaries as Neicy Nash, Brittany Flickinger, Jenna Fredrique, and Loretta Devine.

She is also the proud mother of two daughters whom she hopes will follow in her footsteps as CLD graduates. "I told my daughters that as soon as they reach high school, they will be entering this exact same building learning the same tools I learned because they were very valuable to me," she said.

But of course students do not have to wait until high school to become the next generation of CLD students. Because of CLD's expansion, they can now begin in the fourth grade, which educators say

Gregory W. Porter

is a critical entry point and a time in which kids can begin to create a life plan for success.

Doctor Eugene G. White, former superintendent of Indianapolis Public Schools and current president of Martin University, said he wished there had been a program like the CLD when he was growing up in Lee County, Alabama. As the 2002 recipient of the Accomplished Achievement Award at the Minority Achievers Awards and Scholarship Gala, he said programs such as the CLD takes time with young people, connects them with other achievers in the community—people who look like themselves and gives them a sense of possibility. "It gives them a

2016 CLD Top Ten Feeder Schools

1. **Crispus Attucks Medical Magnet High School**
2. **Pike High School**
3. **North Central High School**
4. **Lawrence North High School**
5. **Warren Central High School**
6. **Lawrence Central High School**
7. **Charles A. Tindley Accelerated School**
8. **New Augusta Public Academy North**
9. **Guion Creek Middle School**
10. **Tindley Collegiate Academy**

sense of hope, shows them what their dreams can be," he said.

A Lasting Legacy

When a child participates in CLD programming, they are not only encouraged to finish high school, graduate college, and remain involved with the Center (whether through financial contributions, alumni activities, or volunteer opportunities), but they are also encouraged to keep their talents close to home. This is something elected officials appreciate. As the chairman of the House Education Committee, Indiana state representative Gregory

Porter is a vocal proponent of the CLD's mission and its desire to flood the state with highly qualified, eligible employees who will be assets to the local community or wherever life takes them.

In addition to encouraging young leaders to think about what success means, there is an overarching lesson of stewardship and community responsibility that is built into the fabric of what the CLD does. It's something that many CLD students such as Jones, Blaine, and others have taken to heart and there are plenty of companies who recognize that commitment and that have shown their support of CLD programs. Second to none in this endeavor has

Joy Mason and Kevin Wade

What parents and area educators have to say about the CLD's impact:

"I really believe in the principles, and I see the affect it has had on my daughter and if it can have that affect, then I know it is a program I want to be a part of."
Yvonne Fitzgerald

"CLD is a great place for our children to come, and it impacts their lives tremendously. It makes a great difference."
Ladonna Emeli

"CLD helps young people become those leaders (who will) keep a free enterprise, capitalistic, and democratic society alive and well in the US of A."
Doctor Perry Clark, former superintendent of Metropolitan School District Lawrence Township Schools.

"There is a drastic difference between kids who are in the program and those who are not . . . they carry themselves differently."
Doctor Jacqueline Greenwood, former principal Arlington High School and CLD board member.

been Lilly Endowment and Eli Lilly and Company, which have been on board with the CLD since the beginning and continue to support its mission.

Derica Rice, executive vice president of global services and CFO of Eli Lilly, said when he visits the CLD he recognizes himself in the young people he meets in the hallways—students who are filled with potential, but need a little push to get them headed in the right direction. When he was asked to serve as a member of the board of directors and become involved with CLD efforts, the decision was not a difficult one to make. As someone who works for a major pharmaceutical company that is not reliant on tangible assets but on brainpower, he believes it is his duty to cultivate the intellect and bright minds that will generate the next new ideas or that next new medicine that might help people. The source of that brainpower is today's young talent so it is not only good for the community, but it is also good for business. "I would encourage all of the other local businesses to be engaged with CLD," Rice said. "Eli Lilly is not the only company in the Indianapolis area that is reliant on future talent, and this is the pool of talent that we will be drafting from, so making that investment today will absolutely pay off for generations to come."

Bill West noted that the CLD's ability to impact multiple generations "shows that it has done something right. When you have parents sending their children to the CLD, schools promoting the program as well as businesses and local organizations who help support the program, then it demonstrates a belief that there is value in what the CLD does and that is so gratifying. We are giving our young people something that they can't get anywhere else."

CLD students visit with Eli Lilly and Company chief financial officer and CLD board member Derica Rice

> "Young people will succeed if they are nurtured, encouraged, and expected to thrive."
>
> *Dennis Bland*

Chapter 10 A Vision for the Future

From its humble beginnings in 1977 to its current place as one of the preeminent youth development programs in the state, the Center for Leadership Development always finds itself in the perfect position to impact young people in an extraordinary way. Motivated by mounting academic and social challenges and a belief that these challenges could be surmounted, CLD organizers worked tirelessly to create an exemplary program of unparalleled distinction. It is something that groups and organizers in Alabama; Georgia; Jackson, Mississippi; and South Bend, Indiana, have noticed and inquired about replicating in their own communities.

"Henry Bundles and the others who were there from the beginning, they got the right people at the right place at the right time and they didn't let their egos get in the way," Holbrook Hankinson said. "That's what makes the CLD so successful. It's people driven. It's community driven. It's more than a program. It's like an extended family."

But the work is far from finished. On January 3, 2017, the CLD celebrated its fortieth anniversary, and with that celebration came the knowledge that there is more work to be done. Today the organization's leaders are more committed than ever to its mission and are determined to make Indianapolis

home to one of the most transformative models in the nation dedicated to the advancement of minority youth. In order to continue empowering young people to believe in themselves, discover their life purpose, and to excel in it, the CLD has created a five-year strategic plan titled "A Center of Hope: Envisioning an Exemplary Youth Experience in Indianapolis," which will help turn their bold vision into a reality.

The plan includes a desire to increase programming participation to 8,000 people per year, provide 15,000 with services, and recruit 30 percent of its participants from high-crime and low-income neighborhoods. The CLD is also exploring adding 15,000 square feet to its building to accommodate planned participation growth. There are also plans for outreach efforts and additional parental/family involvement, as well as creating more awareness. Naturally, this takes time, human talent, and

financial resources, but the CLD remains confident and optimistic about its future.

The CLD is not just another program to save at-risk youth. It is a center of hope where young people are challenged and encouraged to aim high and

excel. It is a place where young people uncover their potential and develop the character qualities that will lead to rewarding and meaningful lives. It is a place that nurtures an abounding pipeline of talented, ambitious young people who are

Helen Baker and Henry Bundles cut cake honoring CLD's fortieth anniversary

Baker and Bundles with current CLD team

graduating high school and college and today are thriving in highly successful careers. And by working in partnership with its stakeholders, the CLD is a place that will be around for a very long time.

"I never thought about it *not* lasting," said Joy Mason (CLD '83). "I know there are some who think that an organization like the CLD should not be relevant in this day and age, but the world is not that utopian. You have to be around as long as you need to be around whether that is thirty, forty, fifty years or more."

For Mason, the idea of attending college was never a question. Both of her parents possessed master's degrees, and she knew she was expected to follow their example. She cannot recall if she first heard about the CLD through the African American community or through her guidance counselors at North Central High School, but when she learned about the Self-Discovery/Career Exploration Project, she signed up for it. To this day, she is glad she did.

"It really is an exacting program," Dennis Bland said. "Over the course of thirteen weeks students hear 'Do it again,' 'Make it better,' and 'Pay attention' more times than they ever have before, but it is with the end goal of helping them succeed and strive for excellence in everything they do."

Even though she knew college was part of her post-secondary plan, Mason said that the CLD exposed her to a variety of career paths she had never considered before. After receiving her high school diploma, she attended Miami University in Oxford, Ohio, where she majored in microbiology. She received her master's degree in pharmaceuticals from Butler University and today is an associate quality consultant at Eli Lilly and Company. She noted that today's teens need the CLD now more than ever and it must be cherished and sustained, expanded, and scaled for the sake of the youth in the community. Thankfully the program has positioned and stewarded itself in such a way that it is ready to launch into the next forty years or more. "As I reflect back on my experiences, career, and the current environment, it hit me that the CLD is even more relevant now," she said. "The world is a crazy place, but the CLD is a place of hope and positivity where young people can grow up to be strong adults with a bright future ahead of them. We must continue to support it."

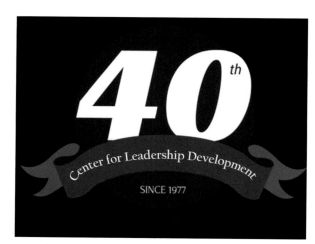

CLD fortieth anniversary logo

Increase Participation/Expand Outreach

Central to the CLD's 2016–20 Strategic Plan is a desire to increase program participation among the young people of central Indiana and beyond. Just prior to the organization's fortieth anniversary, there were 4,000 children and adults taking advantage of more than 8,000 services throughout the year. This multifaceted plan also includes additional objectives, such as:

- Achieving a high school graduation rate of 100 percent.
- Increasing the amount of time CLD students study (more than two hours per night).
- Increasing the number of students served coming from poverty areas.
- Achieving 50 percent increase in reading and math proficiency.
- Increasing the number of counseling services provided to 1,600 annually.

- Increasing the number of CLD alums who enroll in post-secondary programs.
- Increasing the college retention rate of CLD alums.
- Improving curricula and technology to enhance learning and provide better outcomes for CLD students and their families.
- Improving evaluation system to measure program impact.

CLD president Dennis Bland said the Center wants to make sure that every child who utilizes the organization's services has the best opportunity to maximize their God-given talent and potential and, thankfully, there is a diverse staff that helps accomplish that mission. "We believe if they have a breath, a heartbeat, and a pulse they have hope and we are the agents of change that can turn that hope into a reality," he said.

Of course they first must come through the door and that's the second component of the CLD's strategic plan. For years the Center was thought to be an enrichment program for minority children already doing well in school and who only needed a little extra push to get them to the next step. In fact, CLD students literally come from all over the central Indiana area and as the program continues its leaders want to make a point to expand outreach and engage more at-risk youth.

In order to do this, the CLD must increase the number of first-time participants who visit the Center. The CLD is also striving to achieve a 30 percent increase in participation of youth coming from the lowest income households and highest crime areas across Greater Indianapolis. There is so much

How to get involved with the CLD

- Make a 100 percent tax-deductible financial contribution to the CLD and ask an employer if they make matching contributions.

- Serve as a volunteer class facilitator, assist at CLD events, or perform office duties at the Lilly CLD Achievement Center.

- Invite the CLD to give a presentation to a business, organization, or church and spread the word to family, friends, congregation, and neighborhood about CLD programming.

- Partner with the CLD to create an internship program for CLD alums.

- Commemorate a loved one with a contribution to the CLD's In Loving Memory Fund.

- Spread the word about the CLD to other organizations.

- Consider the CLD in your estate planning.

- Join the CLD Alumni Association.

untapped potential in these areas that will continue to be hidden unless these youth and families are handed a light and shown a different possibility for their lives. "We have to develop and implement an annual awareness campaign so that more people hear about the CLD through local and social media so that we can increase our overall program participation by another 5,100 to reach our 8,000 goal," Bland said. "But in order to get the kids involved, you have to help the parents understand the value and benefit of the program."

Mason certainly understands the benefits of the CLD, and she has shared that opportunity with one of her children. In addition to showing her financial support for the organization and staying in touch with the CLD through the alumni association, she was an annual fund cochair for 2015. Quoting Dietrich Bonhoeffer, she said the "test of the morality of a society is what it does for its children," and she feels the CLD is an example of that commitment. "CLD was the first organization I began giving back to as a working adult. I started writing checks right away, even before I was married, because I believed in its mission," she said. "Today, my husband and I continue to do so because it is part of our giving philosophy to support an organization that is doing something important for the youth of the community."

Parental Involvement, Funding, and Community Awareness

In addition to helping parents see the benefits of CLD programming, it is absolutely critical to get them involved. Some of the programs have a required parental participation component, while others do not, but families are always encouraged to be part of the CLD experience so that they can maximize a child's success. "That's one of the reasons we put CLD in a central location," Bland said. "We want to give young people and their parents access to a high quality program at a nominal cost."

The Strategic Plan calls for an increase in the number of parents currently participating in CLD programs, an increase in the number of parents receiving services and workshops from the organization, an increase in the number of parents participating in Center programs for the first time, an increase in parents receiving services for the first time, and to explore the possibility of connecting parents electronically to Parents Chat and other CLD workshops.

Funding and Awareness

In order for the CLD's 2020 Strategic Plan to come to fruition, the Center must increase its annual operating budget from $2 million to $4 million. This goal can be met if the CLD increases its donations by 27 percent, the number of its donors by 25 percent, and increase its grant revenue by $1.44 million. The Center must also cultivate its planned giving donations, increase its number of fundraisers each year, and increase the number of corporate and individual contributions. A particularly great opportunity is for CLD alums to become more actively involved. There are approximately 10,000 alumni such as Jones and Mason, but there is room for many more to give back.

Awareness is the key to helping the CLD accomplish this aspect of the plan, and Bland believes the best way to increase awareness is for the CLD to get the word out and tell people that it is still making an impact on students and families, it is an organization whose value to Indianapolis is increasing, and to showcase their success stories. "It's very important that our alums stay connected to the CLD so that we can track their success and share that information with our donors," he said.

Moving forward

Another part of the CLD's Strategic Plan is to find ways in which the organization can expand. No matter if it is adding new programs to meet additional needs, upgrading technology, expanding the CLD campus with a 14,000-square-foot addition,

CLD board member John Otteson

or replicating the CLD concept in other cities, the Center must continue to move forward.

Mason said that although there is no magic formula to create a winning program such as the CLD, when the right combination of people and purpose comes together, something magical happens. "There will be some zigs and zags and some trial and error, but if you are sincere in your intentions, understand the needs of the local community, and have the proper programs, processes, and procedures in place, there is always opportunity to replicate it or to expand the existing program," she said.

John Otteson was in high school when his father, Schuyler, helped found the CLD, and he is proud to be a second generation of the organization's board of directors. Today, as the market executive/executive director of JPMorgan Chase and Company, he said it is amazing that a group that started as a way to encourage students of color to consider a future in the business arena has grown into such a pillar of the community. He is proud to have such a strong family history with the CLD, but said even if he did not, it would be an organization he would want to be involved with. "Just as the medical community works to combat diseases, the CLD works to combat societal issues that impact us all," he said. "Economic issues have an impact on education, and educational issues have an impact on crime statistics, and the success of our young people have an impact on the success of the city overall."

Otteson believes that Indianapolis was the perfect place in which to launch a program such as the CLD because folks in the community tend to

roll up their sleeves and get to work when they see a need, and he is confident that his late father would be gratified to know that he was part of the early stages of an organization that developed into something really special. "There is still so much to be done though, and we have big plans to take CLD to the next level. It won't be easy, but when you have a group of folks who are willing to work together to serve current students and meet the demands of the next generation, I believe anything is possible," he said.

It is a belief that CLD founding president Henry Bundles shares and one that helps the CLD keep its eye on tomorrow while transforming the children of today. Bundles said:

> We will not be able to progress or grow if we are not prepared and continue to expand our horizons . . . in all things success depends upon previous preparation and without preparation there is sure to be failure. . . . We ask you to contribute to the uplifting of minorities who are less fortunate than you . . . contribute your talents to improve the community. Contribute your time and help organizations whose aim is to help poor people and the disenfranchised have a decent life. Contribute your training and professionalism to cause the right things to happen for society and contribute yourself as a positive image for all people. You can't afford to lose a minute—we have too much at stake.

CENTER FOR
LEADERSHIP
DEVELOPMENT

Empowering Youth ☑ Strengthening Community

A Center of Hope:
*Envisioning an exemplary
youth experience in Indianapolis*

2016–2020 Strategic Plan

CLD Strategic Plan

CENTER FOR LEADERSHIP DEVELOPMENT
MASTER PLAN

AUGUST 2015

arcDESIGN
201 N. Delaware St., Suite B
Indianapolis, IN 46204
T) 317.951.9192
www.arcdesign.us

arcDESIGN
architecture + interiors

CLD Master Plan

"If a community recognizes a problem and envisions a solution, they should go for it."

Steve Stitle

Conclusion

When the Center for Leadership Development began, its founding board members had no way of knowing that the enterprise they launched in the parlor of the Indianapolis Athletic Club would continue to grow and thrive four decades later. They wanted to give minorities the chance to succeed outside of a production line or a secretarial pool. They wanted young people of color to attend college, flourish in the post-secondary environment, to set goals, to have dreams, and know how to make those dreams come true. They wanted to give these students role models who looked like them, offer them the opportunity to see what their future could be, and help them build a solid network of support within the local community.

What started as a plan to engage more minorities in the business community became a means to encourage more minority involvement in every possible career field. The desire to give up-and-coming young people from all walks of life the tools they needed to succeed in their choice of profession became a holistic program that gives an ever-growing range of elementary, junior high, high school, and college students the opportunity to win at life.

Bill West said it was a vision that started it, the human tools that actualized it, individuals such as Henry Bundles, Helen Baker, and Holbrook Hankinson who made it all possible, and the current leadership who keeps it moving forward. "The CLD has been very fortunate because often times the organization is lost when the founding president retires or steps down. Luckily we had Dennis [Bland] step up and help us recast the vision which has led us in new directions we couldn't have dreamed of in 1977," he said.

The CLD's current board chair Tom King said it is amazing to think that what started out as a way to help funnel students of color to the Indiana University School of Business became a cherished program in which nearly every college and university in the state is involved. He said it is an example of what can happen when the black and white communities come together in a spirit of collaboration to create something truly unique. "Everyone knew

CLD Scholars with Helen Baker and Henry Bundles

what their individual roles were and everyone set their egos aside. It was all about the common good and doing what needed to be done to help kids succeed," he said. "Henry had a lot of cache in the community and an expansive network of contacts who had high regard for him. It's amazing the continuity of people who have been involved with the CLD and how they continue to remain engaged for more than four decades."

The CLD is a brand that young people wear as though it were a designer label. It is a calling card that stands for excellence and demonstrates to

guidance counselors, schools, and future employers that these young men and women are learning to set a high bar of achievement for themselves, and that with hard work, persistence, and dedication, nothing will stop them from reaching their life goals.

Over the past forty years the CLD has faced numerous challenges, obstacles, adversities, bumps in the road, and setbacks to emerge as a beacon of hope on the Indianapolis landscape. Today, the organization has fifteen programs, the College Prep Institute, and twenty-four college and university

partners that are awarding a nearly combined $3 million in scholarships annually to CLD students. For this reason the organization is in the superb position to launch forward in a meaningful and holistic way. With more people than ever living at or below the poverty line, it is critical to prepare young people for a future that will demand more of them mentally, physically, financially and spiritually.

"The CLD is not just another youth development program, but a fundamental action plan to create the kind of community we want to see," Bland said. "You can determine what a city will look like based on how well you prepare its young people. When we help the African American and low-income communities aspire for more, we help these young citizens prepare for a challenging environment that will only become more challenging in time. All of the scholarships, college and corporate partnerships, internships, and networking opportunities touch these distinct stakeholders in a succinct and overarching way. Through its innovative programming, the CLD is in the prime position to impact youth, their families, and workforce and by extension, impact the city, the nation, and the world."

Former board chair Steve Stitle said sometimes he worried that the CLD might be the best kept secret in town, but over time he has watched how the

Recognition of all current and former CLD board chairmen

President Dennis Bland speaks at 2017 Awards and Scholarship Gala

organization built its donor base and community partnerships and continues to expand them in such a way that suggests the Center has a broad base of both awareness and reach and making a difference in both the public and private sectors. "The CLD gets results. It's as simple as that and the results aren't merely great, they are phenomenal. Ask twelve CEOs what the CLD has done for the community and you will find that it is preparing kids for life in the workforce, life in the community, and a life of meaningful stewardship. The CLD helps create healthy communities through balanced individuals. What could be better results than that?"

2017 CLD Scholars

Bibliography

"Aiding Minority Business is Goal of New Program." *Indianapolis Star*, March 27, 1970. https://www.newspapers.com/image/107010829/?terms=Minority%2BBusiness%2BDevelopment%2BFoundation%2BHenry%2BBundles.

Allen, Angela. "Leadership Center has Eye on Future." *Indianapolis Star*, March 18, 1991. https://www.newspapers.com/image/106845218/.

Bishop, Reginald. "Testing Business Waters." *Indianapolis News*, October 24, 1977.

Brown, Amos. Center for Leadership Development Radio Broadcast. 2014. WTLC/Radio One. http://praiseindy.hellobeautiful.com/2043809/amos-live-day-at-indy-education-success-story-cld-center-for-leadership-development/.

Center for Leadership Development. "Eli Lilly and Company Foundation Funds Center for Leadership Development." March 19, 2007. http://www.prnewswire.com/news-releases/eli-lilly-and-company-foundation-funds-center-for-leadership-development-52324437.html.

Children's Express. "Leading the Way." *Indianapolis Star*, September 19, 1994. https://www.newspapers.com/image/105127120/?terms=Center%2Bfor%2BLeadership%2BDevelopment.

Center for Leadership Development. College Prep Institute. https://www.youtube.com/watch?v=DwjKphx4-rM.

Center for Leadership Development. Who We Are. https://www.youtube.com/watch?v=i1WZXoSBnjl.

Hooper, Kim. "Organization Nurtures Future Black Leaders." *Indianapolis Star*, October 28, 2003. https://www.newspapers.com/image/127286959/?terms=Dennis%2BBland%2BCLD%2BSuccess%2BPrep.

———. "Success Stories." *Indianapolis Star*, November 28, 1993. https://www.newspapers.com/image/107373003.

Hudnut, William H. III. *The Hudnut Years in Indianapolis, 1976–1991*. Bloomington: Indiana University Press, 1995.

Knight, Dana. "Helen Baker Bundles has Quietly Helped Youth." *Indianapolis Star*, March 10, 2002. https://www.newspapers.com/image/108032998/?terms=Helen%2BBaker%2BBundles.

Knight, Dana. "Stopping Up the Brain Drain." *Indianapolis Star*, March 10, 2002. https://www.newspapers.com/image/108032993.

Knight, Dana. "Eugene G. White Broke Barriers, Made History." *Indianapolis Star*, March 10, 2002. https://www.newspapers.com/image/108032998/?terms=Eugene%2BWhite%2BCenter%2Bfor%2Bleadership.

McFeely, Dan. "A Lot More Room to Build Leaders." *Indianapolis Star*, October 3, 2007.

Merkerson, Fredrick L. "Former CLD Participant Leads Organization into the Future." *Indianapolis Recorder*, August 11, 2000. http://indiamond6.ulib.iupui.edu/cdm/ref/collection/IRecorder/id/97260.

Myrland, John. "Everyone Has Unique Gifts that can be Used to do God's Work." *Pendleton Times-Post*, April 3, 2008. https://www.newspapers.com/image/159837960/?terms=Dennis%2BBland.

Owen, Ken. "Dennis Bland '87 Addresses DePauw's Alumni Reunion Convocation." DePauw University Video. June 11, 2012. https://www.youtube.com/watch?v=3F8NEb85ZeA.

Pierce, Richard. *Polite Protest: The Political Economy of Race in Indianapolis, 1920–1970*. Bloomington: Indiana University Press, 2005.

Smiley, Derwin. "Center for Leadership Development." Derwin Smiley Show. May 1, 2009. https://www.youtube.com/watch?v=YmwxTdw15iw.

Stanczykiewicz, Bill. "The Expectation Factor that Helps Black Youth Achieve." *Indianapolis Star*, May 17, 2004. https://www.newspapers.com/image/127433282/?terms=Success%2BPrep%2BCLD.

Thornbrough, Emma Lou, and Lana Ruegamer. *Indiana Blacks in The Twentieth Century*. Bloomington: Indiana University Press, 2000.

Williams-Gibson, Jessica. "Program Works to Empower Minority Youth." *Indianapolis Recorder*, October 12, 2007. http://www.indianapolisrecorder.com/news/features/article_b516525d-6909-5d96-9863-50b2bb3b7fa1.html.